Faith and Money Relations

Disclaimer

This eBook is provided solely for educational purposes and is not intended to replace professional advice. The author's and views and opinions about financial stability and faith are reflected in the content.

The author and all related contributors have made every effort to ensure that the material in this book is correct and up to date with the latest financial trends and practices. Nonetheless, it is apparent that the financial world changes at a fast speed. Therefore, the author and all other contributors retain the right to revise the content and material supplied in this book when new developments occur. There is no responsibility on the author or any other contributor if there is any outdated information or omissions in this work.

The author and all other contributors accept no responsibility for any subsequent actions taken by all readers because of the materials provided in this eBook, whether monetary, legal, or otherwise. Readers' outcomes will vary depending on how they interpret the contents in this eBook, so no guarantees can be made.

About the Author

Mario R. Andre is an American writer and financial expert. Born and raised in Chicago, IL, Andre comes from a humble background. Having spent a significant amount of his life in the corporate world, he believes that individuals should find and polish their strengths and build on them, rather than working for someone else from nine in the morning to five in the evening. The Bible and the teachings of Jesus Christ has been a constant echo in Andre's life, ever since he decided to bid farewell to the corporate world.

His faith is one of the most important things that inform him professionally and financially. He believes that people should have the courage and the grit to rise, rather than crawling the earth like vermin. He also believes that Jesus was sent to this earth with a mission, and that mission was to free man from all kinds of oppression. He wants his readers to understand the skills and the powers that God has bestowed upon them, and in his opinion, that is the only way they can break the shackles of corporate slavery that feeds off a person's capability and deprives them of their natural ambition.

He wants his readers to achieve financial freedom, which simply cannot come from working a 9-5 job. Andre keeps a keen eye on the latest financial trends and practices, as well as the latest passive income streams that enable a person to become wealthy in the long run, rather than running after riches that can quickly fade away. In the book, he shares his experiences and his knowledge for the betterment of mankind. He also encourages his readers to work hard, while having an unshakable faith in the power of the Lord, since he is the provider and the sustainer of all living things on this earth and beyond.

Preface

The world is a strange place that tries to control the way we think, feel, and perceive. It doesn't value a person's capabilities, talents, wishes, desires, and aspirations. Since birth, we are conditioned into a version of ourselves that is accepted by the people around us. They are the ones who make most of the decisions about how we live, what we choose to study, and how we make a living.

Speaking of making a living, children are made to follow the same "run of the mill" trends of going to college, getting a degree and then working a nine-to-five job. These cycles are passed from one generation to the next, and the sad part is that no one does anything to change these patterns. However, a select few dare to think outside the box, but they are immediately labeled as troublemakers.

Let's suppose you are an immensely gifted and talented individual. People praise you for what you have to offer, but the moment you decide to capitalize on your strengths, the problems begin. We live in a system that thrives on making slaves out of people and depriving them of their birthright to choose what's right for them. Is this something God wishes for us? Absolutely not.

The idea of working a job for a firm is simply outdated, but most regrettably, people are not willing to understand this. When we work a job, we provide our services to a few chosen individuals who get to benefit from our capabilities. Sure, they may provide us with a handsome monthly salary, but is that it? Does a salary determine what we are truly capable of? I don't think so.

Part of the reason why people choose to work these corporate jobs is that it provides them protection. It provides them with the security they are conditioned to seek in life. A job doesn't require risk-taking. It doesn't compel us to step outside our comfort zones. It doesn't encourage us to step into the real world and explore what it has to offer. It doesn't provide us sufficient chances to step outside and discover what we are truly capable of achieving.

In the end, we end up as robots who don't have brains of their own. Robots need a specific level of programming to perform certain tasks, and that is the end of the story. By the time we realize how badly we are being played, we have already missed the train. By the time we choose to look around and find out what we have been missing, we have already lost all of our chances. That is one of the most common reasons why people end up with regrets, self-confidence issues, issues of self-worth, and even mental health problems like depression.

If I can be honest with you, I would say we always have a choice. Sure, the bondage this system uses to control us is too intimidating to break free from. However, if only we have the nerve to stand up for ourselves and make that decision, there is not a single power in the world that can resist us.

I believe we as a group of people lack faith. We lack faith in the power of our Lord and Savior, Jesus Christ. Christ is always with us, watching us, protecting us, and keeping the dangers at bay. It is we who don't believe in him. Do you think he would want his people to live like vermin? No, he doesn't want his people to be slaves to a system. He wants us to be free. Free like birds in the air. It is my firm conviction that the day we decide to step outside our comfort zones, the power of Christ will protect us and will show us the way toward whatever is written in our destiny.

I am also an individual like you all. I come from a broken family where there weren't too many options to choose from. I, too, climbed the nine to five ladder but realized earlier on where it would lead me. I climbed down to pursue my own path and make my own rules along the way. Sure, it wasn't easy. I had to struggle. I had to put the hard yards in, but I can safely say I am happy with where I am now and happy with whatever I have. The real sense of accomplishment comes from the fact that I didn't have to bow down to anyone.

Can I tell you a secret? There is a big difference between being wealthy and being rich. A rich person is the one who has the power to splurge. On the flip side, a wealthy person is one who has enough money to save. Which one would you choose? Would it be alright if you wrote a big check to purchase a brand new Jeep Wrangler while you didn't have 10 cents in your bank account? Or would you rather save up sufficient money to secure your future and the future of your loved ones? Exactly – that's what I thought.

This shimmery corporate lifestyle has made us so addicted to this idea of panache that we are unable to think beyond that. We seek peace only in what's apparent to the world. The only thing that makes us feel whole is being able to flaunt our material gains. Do you really think you can find peace in a material item that is perishable? No, you cannot. At least, Christ doesn't have this idea of peace. This idea has been coined by the people who have laid the foundation of this very system that we live in. The system that feeds us, or so it seems.

The reason why I have written this book is that I want my readers to be adventurous. I want them to be creative, and I want them to think outside the box. My dear friends, I don't want you to back off because of your fear of failure. All of us fear something, but it doesn't mean we should stop trying. Christ has your back, and he will not allow anything to touch you until and unless it is for your own good. I want you, readers, to be financially independent and secure, not because of anyone else, but due to your own grit, courage and ambition.

Table of Contents

Chapter 1: The Difference Between Being Rich and Wealthy

Being rich and being wealthy are two different things, and the difference is hard to discern. Sure, they are often mistaken for one another, but there isn't much common ground between the two. Let's learn the differences before moving on. To put it simply, Robert Kiyosaki once said, "the rich have lots of money, but the wealthy don't worry about money." There couldn't have been an easier way to distinguish between the two.

We see it around us all the time. Doctors, lawyers, bankers, and marketing professionals have a lot to flaunt when it comes to material. They own nice cars, live in comfortable houses, they don the finest brands, but sadly, they fall into the first category. In plain and simple words, they are just rich. The people I have just mentioned are living from one paycheck to the next. Therefore, they don't possess what it takes to amass sufficient assets to fall into the category of the wealthy.

Wealthy people have so much to their name that they don't have to worry about getting up every day and going to work. Sure, they are always on the lookout for active and passive techniques of wealth multiplication, but even if they stop for a month or two, it wouldn't mean anything to them.

Becoming rich without becoming wealthy is all too common. For example, one of the easiest ways to get rich quick is by winning the lottery. Winning a lottery provides you with a quick financial boost, but does it prevent bankruptcies? Absolutely not. The maximum it can do is delay your financial demise, but not eliminate it altogether.

If you asked me if there is a difference between lottery winners or losers, my answer would be "no," there is no difference between the two. The winners also have the same level of assets and unsecured debts as non-winners. Sure enough, becoming wealthy is not the easiest thing to do, but it is possible. All you have to do is use time wisely, and enhance your net worth, so you can avoid the pitfalls of debts and financial insecurity. If you remain patient and attentive, you can create assets that will free you from all financial constraints, and last even after your lifetime.

What Does Being Rich Look Like?

You may disagree with my idea of being rich, and that is perfectly alright. What informs our definition of "richness" has a lot to do with where we live, what we do, and the people who surround us. A person hailing from a poor town where the average annual per capita income of people is $500 will definitely deem a person with a bank balance of $1500 rich. In reality, for a person living in New York, $1500 is not even sufficient enough to cover monthly rent. Here are two common indicators of richness.

Increased Income

What separates rich people from poor people is their high income. A perfect example would be that of a soccer or an NFL player. An average NFL player makes almost $3 million a year, which equates to a little over $500,000 a month. Where will they go if they lose their ability to perform? What if they are shown the door? Do you think they would be able to match such pay if they were to deliver lectures at a community college, or if they joined the police force? They couldn't as they aren't qualified for anything else. This dichotomy makes their riches ridiculously tenuous.

Cost of Spending

There is no bigger enemy of money than aggressive spending. This is a lesson most lottery winners and windfall recipients learn the hard way. The quick influx of money often makes a person feel richer than he really is.

Consequently, these lottery winners end up with destructive spending habits and financial mismanagement. The money they spend is usually hard to replace. Don't get me wrong. Not all rich people spend recklessly. Some of them are very mindful of their expenditures, and that is a good thing.

However, promotions and business success oftentimes compel people to upgrade their lifestyles to something that is harder to sustain. Despite their elevated financial status, they are no better than they were with limited means. The story remains the same.

What Does Being Wealthy Look Like?

Wealth is the overall count of income-generating assets a person owns, rather than money. Studies have shown that in America, a person needs to have $2.4 million to be regarded as "wealthy." Interestingly, wealth, just like riches, is relative. For example, it might take a lot more to maintain a comfortable lifestyle in New York, as opposed to the Great Plains.

Investments and Passive Income

Usually, wealth comes from investments and passive income sources. According to the IRS, wealth is what you make out of anything that you earn without active participation. Some common examples include royalties, stock dividends, rental income, and real estate.

Financial Freedom

Passive income sources give birth to financial freedom. This freedom allows you to live your life on your own terms, without having to move a muscle. Different people have different approaches to financial freedom. While some opt for a frugal lifestyle, others choose to accumulate more than they are able to spend. The moment you attain financial freedom is the moment you are free from all financial worries. When that happens, you set out in pursuit of goals that aren't linked to money in any way.

I don't know why I am quoting so much from Robert Kiyosaki, but the old man has a point. He says, ***"Rich is quantified in money, whereas wealth is measured in time, and not in Dollars."*** To put it simply, wealth determines how long you will be able to maintain a lifestyle.

How to Become Wealthy

Sure, we will discuss this over the course of this book, but here is a quick overview. The first step towards being wealthy is not focusing on your monthly paycheck. While it is your bread and butter, it shouldn't take away from you your birthright to dream big. Moreover, steer clear of schemes that promise you instant wealth. The steps I am sharing with you will help you break free from debt, and enable you to look at investment options.

Start Saving

It doesn't matter how insignificant your paycheck is. You should try your best to save a small trifle from your salary every month. Let's say 10-15% of your salary should end up in savings. To make your life easier, you can open up a separate bank account to set aside your savings. This will help you save, without thinking too much about it. If you find saving difficult, take a close look at your budget. You might have to get rid of some expenses.

Pay Off High-Interest Debts

Being debt-free is one of the things that distinguish the rich and the wealthy. If you want wealth, you need to get rid of your debt. Debt and wealth can stay in the same place. Start by paying off high-interest debts. Your credit card is a great example. Also, do some research to find out whether or not it is a good idea to refinance a student loan or mortgage at a better interest rate. You should also explore paths to student debt freedom. Leading a debt-free life should be your number one priority if you want to embark on a journey towards wealth.

Focus on Investments

As difficult as it seems, investment is the quickest way to being wealthy. Sure, there are risks involved, but there are plenty of options out there. You can either resort to an automated advisor, seek financial advice from a broker, or invest in stuff outside the stock market. You can also invest in assets or a high-yielding savings account. By doing these things, you will make your money work for you.

Eliminate Unnecessary Expenditures

The easiest way to grow your wealth is to stay within your means. Instead, it is better to live a bit below your means. This way, you will save more and invest, which will provide you with bigger returns in the long run. Living within or below your means is all about resisting the urge to splurge on designer clothes or the brand new iPhone when you have a perfectly functioning smartphone to serve the purpose. Only buy the things you genuinely need, and not the things you want.

What Are Your Long-Term Financial Goals?

Unlike a rich person, a wealthy person builds assets and has long-term financial goals to focus his efforts on. When the going gets tough, ask yourself what you set out to achieve in the first place. Is it temporary comfort or luxury, or do you want to lay the foundation of financial success that your generations will profit from, even when you are not around? Very good! That's what I thought.

Wealth Comes from Your Mind

As we have already discussed, being wealthy doesn't mean having a wallet stuffed with fresh dollar bills. Sure, I wouldn't mind a wallet filled with cash, but there is more to it. Wealth is actually a mindset. A person who is wealthy or at least plans to be wealthy in the future has some long-term goals that continue to drive him.

Just ask yourself a question, and answer it honestly. Wouldn't it be amazing to retire early, with a couple of houses to your name? Wouldn't it be great to travel to your favorite destination with your family and friends, whenever you want? While you should work hard at your job, your salary shouldn't dictate your financial goals. You should have ample savings and investments that could last you a couple of lifetimes.

Some Examples of Wealthy and Rich People

The current net worth of Warren Buffett is $80.8 billion. On the flipside, the net worth of Jeff Bezos is $145 billion. Therefore, Buffet is known as a frugal billionaire. Buffet still lives in his Nebraska home. He bought this property back in 1958 for $31500. In 1971, he bought a California beach house for $150,000. He sold his California beach house for $7.5 billion[1], so can you dig it?

There was a time when MC Hammer[2], the American Rapper had $30 million in his bank account. He also owned a $1 million house with hundreds of staff members. He even had 19

---

[1] Madeline Stone, M. S. (2018, October 15). Warren Buffett's Southern California vacation home. Business Insider. Retrieved October 15, 2018, from https://www.businessinsider.com/photos-of-warren-buffetts-house-in-california-2017-2?IR=T

[2] Matthew Michaels, M. M. (2019, August 8). Celebrities who were rich and famous. Business Insider. Retrieved August 8, 2019, from https://www.businessinsider.com/rich-famous-celebrities-who-lost-all-their-money-2018-5?IR=T#despite-his-hit-u-cant-touch-this-mc-hammer-filed-for-bankruptcy-9

racehorses in his stable. Sadly, due to aggressive spending, he lost all of his money. In 1996, Hammer was declared bankrupt. As a result, he ended up in debt of $13 million.

Wrapping It Up

Before we move to the next chapter, I am assuming you have gotten an idea of how different it is to be wealthy, as opposed to being rich. While rich people spend, wealthy people save and invest. Wealthy people have a lot of money, but they don't spend it in a single go.

Furthermore, wealthy people run away as far as possible from wealth. They don't use debt until and unless it is something substantial as buying property. Instead of spending all of their cash, a wealthy person takes cash and transforms it into assets. Surprisingly, wealthy people might lead a more frugal life than most rich people, but they aren't dependent on a paycheck.

Chapter 2: The Difference between Passive and Active Income Streams

Income falls into two basic categories, i.e., passive and active. While most people have heard of the two terms, they aren't sure of how different they are from one another. Moreover, not many people are clear on ways to generate passive income. First of all, people don't know much about passive income, and secondly, even if they do, it is the belief that understanding passive income is the key to financial independence and well-being.

Pardon me for quoting Robert Kiyosaki once again, but I can't help it. According to him;

"The ability or aptitude to transform earned money into passive income and/or portfolio income is the key to financial freedom and huge wealth,"

Active Income

As the name implies, active income is the amount of money you receive for providing a specific service, like working a job. Salaries, commissions, and tips are all examples of active income. Other kinds of active income include self-employment, and material participation in business.

In most cases, you need a steady active income stream to be able to generate passive income. Take real estate investors, for example. Before they can invest in real estate, they need to have an active income stream. This is part of the reason why most real estate investors work a part-time job. They accumulate as much money as possible, so they are able to invest in things like rental properties.

Let's talk about some of the ways to earn active income. Hourly wages are one of the most common types of active income, whether they come from full-time or part-time employment. The good thing about hourly pay is that you get to make extra money by working overtime, on the weekends and holidays.

Salary is different from an hourly wage. A salary is a fixed amount of money that you receive after working a regular schedule. People who receive an active salary trade 40 hours a week for a guaranteed and fixed amount of income.

Another form of active income is commissions. However, the amount of money received can vary, depending upon the work done. A great example is that of real estate agents. A real estate agent may receive a commission of 3-6% for selling a house. Moreover, a leasing commission will amount to one month of rent. However, people who work a straight commission often find their commissions rising and falling. It all depends upon the number of deals closed, as well as what time of the year it is.

Then there are tips. Tips are also a kind of active income that one receives depending upon the services provided. The recipients of these tips are the people working in the restaurant or hospitality industries. These people earn an hourly or monthly wage, while the tips come exclusively from satisfied customers.

Consultation income and freelance fees are two other forms of active income. Nowadays, people with digital marketing, content writing, graphic designing, and web designing skills are highly demanded. These people can start a freelancing business and work as independent contractors for their clients.

Passive Income

As the name implies, passive income is the amount of money that comes from an income-generating asset in which the investor isn't directly involved. In most cases, such assets are bought using money from active income. The great thing about passive income is that people not only get to save time and energy, but they also don't have to pay Medicare or social security tax, along with other deductions.

Now, let's look at some examples of passive income.

Interest income is a common example of passive income streams. One can generate interest income by owning a bond or investing their savings in a deposit certificate. Most regrettably, the interest rate paid on investments is usually less than the rate of inflation. As a result, an investor can lose principal by investing in assets that pay passive interest income.

Another source of passive income are the dividends of publicly traded stocks. MasterCard, Apple and Nike are some of the blue chip companies that pay dividends. However, just like an interest income, dividends coming from a big company are often low. In fact the S&P 500 Dividend Yield has come down from 1.93% to 1.35%.

If you are looking for another steady way of earning passive income, you can be a silent partner and make limited partnership earnings from a real estate business or real estate. Such investments have a higher potential return due to the recurring income. Moreover, you also get to enjoy a profit percentage if the business is sold.

As charming as they seem, higher returns also come with a higher amount of risk. If you invest in a limited partnership business as a silent partner, chances are you will lose all of your investment if things go wrong.

Rental income is one of the safest forms of passive income. Rental income from real estate offers a steady risk-adjusted return, along with the potential profit that comes from the appreciation of property upon sale.

Studies have shown that since the last recession in 2007, the median price of house sales has increased by 67%. Moreover, single family rents have also increased. Another single family trends report on rental investment has revealed that in recent times, rent growth in occupied and vacant single family homes has increased by 8.3%.

However, historically speaking, real estate markets tend to go up and down. For example, prior to the recession, the prices of homes fell between 2007 and 2009. At that time, a lot of property owners lost their properties to real estate foreclosures. At the same time, real estate investors started purchasing short sales, as well as REO properties from banks.

Generating Income from Real Estate

Interestingly, with real estate, you can earn an active income, a passive income, and sometimes, a combination of the two. The nature of income, whether it is active or passive, depends heavily on the investor's strategy. Another factor to consider is whether or not the investor wants to generate potential income over a short or long term.

Active Real Estate Income

There are investors out there that flip and wholesale properties. Such investors are looking to make short term income. What happens typically is that an investor purchases a property that needs repairs for a lower price. They then proceed to make some necessary upgrades, and then sell the same property at a profit. Therefore, such investors are known as flippers. They make quick upgrades to the property, and then sell it at a higher price, before market conditions change.

The great thing about wholesalers is that they can identify property that is undervalued. Once they have identified such a property, they get it under contract. Then, the purchasing contract is assigned to an investor against a small wholesale fee. Working with a real estate wholesaler is good for a number of reasons. First of all, it allows you to identify off-market deals that provide instant equity, once the necessary repairs have been made.

However, there is a significant amount of risk involved in generating active income from real estate. Moreover, it is somewhat similar to working a full time job. There are times when there aren't any properties available to flip and wholesale opportunities start drying up. As a result, the active income from real estate also starts to decline.

Passive Real Estate Income

Passive real estate income is earned by buy-and-hold investors. It happens in two different ways, which are as follows.

- Recurring net income after rents from the tenants have been collected, and all the necessary repairs have been made, and the bills have been paid.
- Secondly, when appreciation is earned upon the sale of the property.

Some financial experts refer to passive income from real estate sources as making money, while taking a nap. According to the famous political economist, John Stuart Mill:

"Landlords amass wealth while sleeping, without working, risking, or saving."

To be very honest, if you want to make passive income from real estate, you will have to do some work. Even if all the details of rental property management have been assigned to a local property manager, you have to stay on top of the whole process.

Let's suppose there is a passive real estate investor who regularly reviews financial statements such as cash flow reports and income statements. Moreover, he also pays periodic visits to remote investments outside the state. He is also on the lookout for new ways to grow rental properties, while growing his portfolio.

The good thing about passive real estate income is that an investor can spend as little time on his business as possible. On the other hand, when an active real estate investor stops working, they also stop making money. They have to work tirelessly to make a living. This is the reason why most real estate investors deploy the passive approach towards real estate investments.

Taxing Passive and Active Incomes

Another amazing benefit of making passive income from real estate is the preferential tax treatment that comes from passive income. The IRS looks at making a fixed salary from a 9-5 job, as well as flipping real estate as earned income. The problem with earned income is that it is subject to Medicare and FICA taxes that amount up to 15.3%, when you attain a certain level of income. Moreover, when the property is held for less than a year, short term gains from wholesaling or flipping real estate are also taxed. Moreover, people who earn an active income also have limited opportunities, when it comes to using tax deductions for a reduction in the amount of paid income tax.

Passive income isn't just subject to FICA taxes. However, on the bright side, there are various ways investors can protect their passive income from higher effective tax rates. For example, a passive real estate investor can claim the following deductions.

- Maintenance and repairs
- Property taxes
- Mortgage interest payments
- Depreciation
- Property management fees

Long term capital gains tax at the time of investment property sale is either 0%, 15% or 20%. It all depends on the investor's level of taxable income, as well as their filing status. Moreover, even if the investor falls within the 32% federal income tax bracket or higher, the highest capital gains tax would cap at 20%.

Chapter 3: Assets and Liabilities

The two most important components of corporate balance sheets and financial statements are assets and liabilities. While there are several ways to distinguish between the two, let's take a simple approach.

What Is an Asset?

An asset can be any good or resource that is used for cash flow generation. Furthermore, an asset minimizes expenses, offering future economic benefits for businesses, governments and individuals. Assets tend to have a specific economic value, which is good for a number of reasons. It increases a business's value, and the net worth of an individual. From a company's viewpoint, assets also facilitate operations.

Personal assets are the ones owned by an individual. On the flipside, business assets are the ones owned by a corporation Moreover assets can appear in a physical, as well as an intangible form. Sometimes, they can be sold right away, while in some cases, they are available for a long time. To calculate the solvency, equity or general financial health of a business, you must subtract the total number of liabilities from the cumulative sum of assets. Liabilities include accounts payables as well as outstanding debts.

What Is a Liability?

When it comes to bookkeeping, financial obligations to external parties are called liabilities. The most common example of a small business corporate liability is the monetary debt. They are mentioned under the account payable section on a company's cash flow statement.

Liabilities are further broken down into two categories, i.e., short-term liabilities and long-term liabilities. The first category needs to be paid off within a year. Whereas, long term liabilities must be paid in a little over a year. Then, there is another small category known as contingent liabilities. These liabilities are payable only in certain conditions. Some of the most common examples of liabilities include credit card debt, machinery depreciation, income tax, sales tax etc.

Assets and Liabilities: Are They Relatable?

Assets make up for a net gain in value, whereas liabilities lead to a net loss. The standard accounting equation is used to compare the total assets of the company to the total liabilities. Investors on the other hand, use this equation for the valuation of the company in general. On the balance sheet, assets are listed on the left side of the page. Depending upon the standard accounting functions of a company, the assets column might contain current as well as fixed assets. The right side contains all the long term and short term liabilities.

Six Different Types of Assets

Here are the assets that appear on the balance sheet.

Current Assets

As the name implies, current assets are extremely fluid in nature, and therefore, they can be sold at any given time. Some of the most liquid assets are bonds, stocks, mutual funds, cash, as well as other marketable securities. The interesting thing about liquid assets is that their price doesn't fluctuate, even if they are sold. On the business end, current assets include cash, account receivable, prepaid expenses and inventory.

Fixed Assets

Fixed assets are also known as hard assets, and sometimes long term assets. The reason why they are called hard assets is that they take longer to earn a cash value, and therefore, they lack the liquidity found in current assets. They cannot be sold at their desired value, as quick as current assets. Some common examples of fixed assets are land, furniture, machinery, and other assets that aren't intended for sale within one year.

Intangible Assets

It is a bit confusing, but tangible assets are the ones that might exist in theory, but not practically. Some common examples of intangible assets are intellectual properties, permits, brand repute, patents, and trademarks. These assets can have a huge boost in value, depending upon their successful use.

Tangible Assets

As the name implies, these assets are real property. Some common examples of tangible assets include real estate, inventory and cash. These items can be physically used, and they remain within the passion of the owner. Most tangible assets fall within the category of current assets.

Operating Assets

Operating assets are the ones that generate value through everyday operations, while enabling a business to streamline the workflow. Some common examples of operating assets are inventory, licenses, machinery and copyrights.

Non-Operating Assets

Unlike operating assets, non-operating assets aren't used for day to day business activities, but their existence surely adds value to the business. Some examples are short-term investments and vacant pieces of land.

Some Common Asset Examples

A well-organized corporation has assets in all areas of the business. Some common examples are as follows.

Cash

The ultimate short term asset is cash. Not only is cash financially flexible, but it also helps businesses act upon financial setbacks.

Intellectual Properties

As discussed above, intellectual properties fall within the category of long term assets. A company with high quality copyrighted material and patents is more likely to bag success in the future.

Real Estate

As we know, Real estate comes under potentially flexible assets. The great thing about real estate is that it tends to appreciate with age. By owning a piece of land or some buildings, a business can make handsome revenue in the future, if it chooses to sell pieces of its real estate. In the short term, a company can also borrow cash against its real estate. However, the bank loan it receives will lead to a long term liability, despite allowing the business to fulfill urgent financial obligations.

Machinery

Machinery is an asset that assists a business in day to day activities. The sad part is, machinery tends to depreciate with time. However, a business always has the option to claim their depreciations in the form of tax deductions.

Intangible Assets

Interestingly, intangible assets can result in employee retention[3]. A strong organizational culture, unlike other assets, cannot be bought or sold in the marketplace. However, it does compel talent to stay within the company for a long time, while the company continues to benefit from their competencies and their professional prowess.

Some Common Examples of Liabilities

Just like assets, liabilities also appear in all nooks and corners of a business.

Payments to Lenders

The good thing about taking loans is that it enhances short-term liquidity. However, these loans can result in long term liability, if not paid soon enough.

Annual Income Tax

Annual income tax falls within the category of short term liability. Such taxes are to be paid once a year, but theoretically, they fall under short term liabilities.

---

[3] MA, M. (2022, February 25). Employee Retention Guide. Masterclass.Com. Retrieved February 25, 2022, from https://www.masterclass.com/articles/employee-retention-guide#quiz-0

Unearned Liability

In some cases, the income statement[4] of a business shows a revenue deficit. Such a deficit is a short term liability. At the start of a financial year, companies predict a certain level of cash flow. When that level isn't met, the deficit appears on the right side of the balance sheet, where the liabilities are.

[4] MasterClass, M. A. (2021, November 4). Income Statement Written by the MasterClass staff. MasterClass. Retrieved November 4, 2021, from https://www.masterclass.com/articles/how-to-read-and-understand-an-income-statement#quiz-0

Chapter 4: Best Passive Income Streams in 2022

Whether you run a side business or want to make some extra money, passive income techniques are worth a try. While they keep you financially fit during good times, they can also have your back in tough circumstances if you get fired or your business goes bankrupt. The best thing about passive income is that it provides you with the financial security that you want in life.

Moreover, you can make some passive income while running a business or working a 9-5 corporate job. Furthermore, passive income streams also allow you to accumulate sufficient wealth for your retirement plans. Even if you are out of a job, passive income streams can enable you to send your kids to good colleges while maintaining a decent lifestyle.

Let's Define Passive Income

In simple words, passive income is the money that comes from an independent source that has nothing to do with your employer. According to the IRS, passive income comes from two primary sources. The first one is real estate, while the second one is any business activity that you are not directly a part of.

Some common examples are royalties from paid books or stock dividends.

Contrary to popular belief, with passive income streams, you don't get paid for no work. Sure, it is not as hectic as working a job or running a business, but it requires some upfront efforts. To keep your passive dollars coming in, you still have to keep your rental property in top shape or your product updated. However, if you commit to it with all seriousness, passive income offers the stability and the security that you want from life.

Passive Income Ideas for Building Wealth

Rental Income

Rental properties are great for making passive income, but it needs a lot more work than you expect. If you don't learn to convert it into a profitable venture, chances are you will lose your investment. However, to make good money off a rental property, here are a few things you must determine earlier on.

- Your expected return on the investment.
- The cost and expenses on the rental property.
- The financial risks of property ownership.

Let's suppose you want to make $10000 a year from your rental property, while the property has a monthly mortgage of up to $2000, and you have to pay $300 in costs. You will have to charge a rent of more than $3000 each month to reach your annual goal.

However, there are some risks involved. Here are a few questions you need to answer before getting into rental properties.

- Does your property have a market?
- What if your tenant pays late or damages the property in some way?
- What if you fail to rent out your property?

Any of the aforementioned factors can affect your passive income goals attached to this rental property. Moreover, economic downturns can present you with some challenges. For example, while your tenants fail to pay on time, you will still have to pay your mortgage. In some cases, the price of the property might just go up due to low mortgage rates.

Furthermore, there are also scenarios where the rent coming from the tenants is insufficient to pay the mortgage. To protect your investment, you will have to factor in all of these possibilities.

Affiliate Marketing

Affiliate marketers appear in different forms. Sometimes they are bloggers, while sometimes, they are influencers. Their job is to promote somebody else's product by adding a link to their website, which redirects visitors to the other party's website.

Amazon, eBay, and Awin are some of the most popular affiliate platforms. Social media platforms like Instagram and TikTok have also emerged on the scene. They help influencers promote products and services to final consumers.

As an affiliate marketer, you can add an email list to your blog for enhanced following, or you can direct visitors to specific products and services they are looking for. So, is there a big opportunity? Of course there is.

When a visitor clicks and purchases on a third-party affiliate website, the site owner makes a commission. The commission you earn equates to 3-7% of the actual price of the product. But to make this much income on your website, you will have to generate a decent amount of traffic. Moreover, you will have to stick to a specific niche to make a serious amount of money.

Affiliate marketing falls within the passive category since all you have to do is add a link to your website. However, if you can't attract the right kind of traffic, you are doomed for failure. The best way to do so is to update your blog with organic and well-researched content to your blog for better SEO.

There is, of course, some risk involved. If you are new to this method of money-making, you will have to spend some time getting the hang of the affiliate ecosystem. Moreover, you will have to work hard researching content ideas to attract organic traffic. It gets even worse, when your hard-earned traffic bounces off to the next influencer or blogger. You can either switch to paid SEO activities or spend some time building your business organically. Organic techniques are beneficial in the long run.

Course Creation

Another great passive income stream is course creation. You have to design audio or video courses and then kick back while the money rolls in from your product sales. Some popular course-sharing sites are Coursera, Udemy, and SkillShare.

The best thing to do would be to adopt a free model. What happens typically is that you offer free content until you cultivate a strong following on any of these platforms. Once you have the traffic you need, you can then start charging money for additional content. Providing free content gives your audience a glimpse of your expertise. Therefore, they are compelled to pay more. Language teachers and stock picking experts often deploy this technique.

The big opportunity is that this income stream helps you make easy money in a limited amount of time. However, the risk is, it takes a lot of time and effort to create a single course. Moreover, your content should be organic, well researched, and informational in every way. If it fails to add value, it won't sell, and all of your efforts will go in vain.

Furthermore, you have to be consistent with your approach. You need to bombard your audience with valuable content. You cannot expect to make a decent amount of money with just one course. On the bright side, once you master this business model, making money won't be much of an effort.

EBook Writing

The great thing about eBook writing is the low publication cost and the extensive distribution capabilities of platforms like Amazon. Amazon's distributive prowess can easily expose your book to millions of global buyers.

To be able to write and sell eBooks, you need to have expertise in a specific area. Moreover, you also need to be equipped with skills and capabilities that not many writers have. With online platforms, you can easily design a comprehensive book in no time. You can even test-market different price points, as well as different titles.

However, just like designing online courses, you need to put out a significant number of eBooks that can click with the readers. Not only will it cultivate a following, but it will also strengthen your credibility in the market.

If we talk about opportunities, eBooks are great not only for delivering valuable information to the readers, but they can also divert attention to other items that you have on offer. Some examples include seminars, courses, and other eBooks on a variety of topics.

However, there are some risks involved. First of all, your eBook should be flawless, and secondly, you must be able to market it on podcasts and other websites. Therefore, you have to put in a lot of upfront effort to earn your remuneration.

On the bright side, eBooks are great when it comes to exhibiting your industry expertise. If you can pull it off, these eBooks will help you enhance other areas of your business. The biggest risk is that you will have to spend a lot of time and energy on a little reward.

Selling Photography Online

Selling photography over the internet is by far the easiest passive income stream and also the most obvious one. However, it can surely scale your efforts if you can sell the same image over and over again. To do this, you will have to partner with companies like Getty Images, Alamy, Shutterstock, or Pexels.

To begin with, you need approval from the platform. Once the approval is there, you can provide them with your images, so people can download them and use them for creative purposes in blog posts as well as social media content. The platform will pay you every time a person downloads one of your images.

However, you need to provide the platform with images that appeal to a specific audience and represent a particular scene. If you talk about creativity, the possibilities are endless. You can use models to promote a specific item, or you can capture picturesque sceneries with your camera. You can even capture real-life events.

The biggest opportunity with selling or licensing your images is that it allows you to scale your efforts. It gets even better when you provide images that will be high in demand for quite some time. It is even possible to sell the same image hundreds and thousands of times, depending upon how many people need them and how many times they are needed.

If we talk about risks, your biggest strength can become your biggest failure. For example, you can provide Getty Images with hundreds of images, while none of them would make meaningful sales. Only a few of them might provide the results you are looking for. Therefore, you have to be consistent and continue to provide them with images on a regular basis.

As a photographer, you need to go out on the field to capture new images all the time. Then, you have to process them, so they appear flawless in every way to drive your revenue. Furthermore, motivation is also difficult to maintain. While some images could be your lottery ticket, some of them might never sell. There is a lot of trial and error involved, but if you are persistent and receptive enough, success will come your way.

Creating Applications

App creation is a field of work that needs upfront time investment, while it pays off in the long haul. Your app could be anything. It could be a game or something that allows businesses to streamline their day-to-day work activities. Once your application is public, users will download it, and you will get to earn.

If you can design something that appeals to your target audience, you can make a fortune. The trick is to figure out the best ways to generate sales from the application you have created. You can run ads within the app, or you can charge a nominal fee upon each download. If your app becomes popular, you will have to tweak some features to keep it relevant.

The biggest risk is that app creation needs a lot of time which often creates a lack of profitability. You can either choose not to invest too much money in the application to protect yourself from potential downsides or vice versa. However, it is better to invest in the project because it is a competitive market out there, and your inability to add value can go against you. But at the same time, it can result in loss too.

Moreover, you need to make sure if your app collects any bits of information, it complies with the privacy standards, which tend to differ from one region to the next. Furthermore, the popularity of an application can dry out pretty easily, thus sending your cash flow to the abyss. You need to upgrade the app to stay relevant.

Flip Retail Products

Online sales platforms like eBay and Amazon can also come in handy. All you have to do is to find items at cut-rate prices and sell them on these platforms. You'll be able to make a handsome profit on these platforms. You might even cultivate a loyal following of customers that track your deals. The great opportunity is that you can always find people that can help you access goods at discounted prices. You can also find valuable merchandise that people might have overlooked.

The risk is, while it is easy to materialize this strategy online, it is not always easy to find a regular supply of merchandise. Furthermore, you need to invest a significant amount of money in the products you intend to sell. Therefore, you will need a robust amount of cash. Moreover, you'll have to know the market, so you don't buy at a higher price. Similarly, you can also end up with products with little or no demand.

REITs

A real estate investment trust or REIT is an organization that manages and owns real estate. The legal structure of such companies keeps them from paying little or no tax, provided they extend all of the income of shareholders.

If we talk about opportunities, a REIT can be purchased on the stock market, just like any other business. You'll get the opportunity to earn each dividend the company pays out. Furthermore, most stable and reputable REITs are known for increasing their dividend amount per annum. Therefore, with time you will have a growing dividend stream.

Just like dividend stocks, an individual REIT can be riskier than owning an ETF with several REIT stocks. For diversification, all you need is a fund, which makes it safer than purchasing individual stocks, and you might even get a decent payout.

Speaking of risks, it takes a lot of time to analyze each REIT, to pick a good one. Moreover, you might even lose money in the process if you don't know what you are doing. Like any other stock, the stock prices can fluctuate at any time. Furthermore, REITs are not free from difficult economic times. If the REIT fails to generate sufficient income, it might just have to cut the dividend or eliminate it altogether. Consequently, your passive income stream will take a hit when you may need it the most.

Sponsored Social Media Posts

If you have a strong following on social media, you can leverage that following and make money. All you have to do is to partner with growing consumer brands. Place, endorse, and integrate those products into your content, and the companies will pay you for your influencer efforts. The trick is to be consistent with your efforts and share posts regularly.

Using your social media presence is a great business model in today's time. While you'll continue to receive clicks on your posts, you'll have a good chance of monetizing your content by setting up sponsored social media posts from the brands that attract your followers.

However, there is some risk here as well. First of all, you will need a large and loyal following. If you don't have a healthy following, brands won't take the risk of investing in you. When it comes to marketing, growing businesses don't have the margin of failure to try out new things until and unless they are 100% sure that they will deliver their KPIs. Furthermore, you might spend time and resources trying to create valuable content, only for them to go in vain.

Create a Blog or a YouTube Channel

Are you a footballer extraordinaire, virtuoso guitarist, or a cooking expert? It's time to make some money from your passions or your hobbies. YouTube is a great place to showcase your talent and make money by running ads for businesses within or outside your niche. You can even start a blog on your website where you can charge money for extra content.

Blogs and YouTube channels, despite their potential profitability, are long-term strategies. In the beginning, you have to put out a decent amount of content. Once you make a name for yourself, money can start rolling in, quicker than you can imagine.

The big opportunity with blogs and YouTube channels is that the more unique your message is, the higher your likelihood of making it big. Once you cultivate a large following, you can monetize your content. When that happens, brands will start taking an interest in you, and you will get the ads you need to grow.

However, there are some downsides to this strategy. Let's suppose you invest a significant amount of time and energy into making content. All of a sudden, it will dawn upon you that there is only a small percentage of the population that is interested in what you talk about. This can be very frustrating for a content creator. Your content should resonate with a larger number of people if you want it to be profitable.

Your area of interest might have a niche market, but it is still too early to predict anything conclusively. With digital, you never quite know whether or not something will click until it is live. Therefore, you have to be a little experimental before giving up altogether. Take calculated risks, and don't shy away. You never know when your moment may come.

Minimizing Taxes on Passive Income Streams

A passive income stream is a great side hustle. However, with these passive income streams come tax liabilities. There are ways to minimize your taxes, though. You can set yourself up as a business, or you can create a retirement account. It is worth noting that this strategy won't apply to all passive income strategies. Here is what you need to do.

- First of all, you have to register with the IRS, and you will receive a tax identification number for the business.
- Next up you can get in touch with a broker to open up a self-employed account for your retirement.
- You also have to determine the kind of retirement account that is most suitable for you.

Two of the most popular options in this regard are the SEP IRA and the solo 401(k). If you put your cash in either of the two accounts, you can enjoy some tax breaks on your annual taxes. The great thing about the 401(k) is that you can stuff all of your earnings into that account up to the annual maximum. On the flip side, the SEP IRA only allows a 25% contribution. Moreover, the 401(k) allows you to contribute 25% of your annual profits as well.

Sell Handmade Goods

Now this one needs some artistry, but if you can pull it off, you can make good money off of it. Is there a craft you are good at? Maybe you are good at woodcraft. If you are then you are in luck. You can make wooden decoratives or small pieces of furniture and sell them online. You can also make hand-woven rugs, or decoratives with some beautiful glasswork.

There is no limit to creativity, and if you are a creative person with a hidden talent, your options are endless. You may not realize this, but if there was a better time to be on the internet, that time is now. At the moment, the internet is home to more than 4.6 billion people. Therefore, the internet is the perfect place to build and scale your business. Moreover, there are many amazing websites where you can sell your products.

Interestingly, there are sites that have specific niches for users to choose from. If you want to be an entrepreneur that dabbles in handicrafts, you can always try out websites like Amazon, eBay, AliExpress and Ruby Lane. You can even set up your own unique website, and use it as an ecommerce platform.

Rent Out Your Vehicle

It might sound a little strange at first but of all the things that we have discussed so far, your car is the perfect that can make you a healthy amount of passive income. You can put your car up for rent, and make money off of it. Moreover, in this digital age, you don't have to use word of mouth to sell your car, or advertise in the newspapers. Sure, you can do all those things, but wouldn't it be amazing to do those things through your phone.

That's right ladies and gentlemen. There are online platforms that allow car owners to put their vehicles up for rent. Turo is one such platform. Chances are you have been using your UBER. If you are, you can check out tools like Wrapify or Carvertise. By using these tools, you won't have to ride around in your car sharing rides, and let someone else do the driving for you. You can utilize all of that time doing something productive.

Lend Money to Your Peers

Do you have some extra cash lying around? Well you are in luck. You can use all of that money to generate some extra income for yourself. The easiest way to do so is by giving out loans from that access money to your peers. It sounds weird, but peer to peer lending can actually be a valuable side hustle.

Contrary to popular belief, you don't have to lend specifically to your friends and colleagues, you can invest all or a portion of your cash into a small business, and wait for the profits to come. If you want to expedite the process, you can simply use online tools like Prosper, LendingClub or Worthy. These online platforms help potential borrowers meet lenders.

Such platforms entertain loan requests, while the interest rate is determined based on the borrower's identity. You can end up with an interest rate of five to six percent, depending upon who your borrower is, what they do, and what is their current credit condition.

Make Money While Shopping Online

That's right; it is possible to make money while shopping online. There are some online stores that can help you do that. Moreover, after signing up, you don't have to do anything for them except shopping. The more you shop, the more points you will gain, and you will utilize these points for future purchases, while saving money.

A word of advice, try not to exceed your monthly shopping limit. Moreover, you can also max out your credit card in a bid, as it will help you win a reward or two. Some of the most popular online shopping platforms are Rakuten, MyPoints and SwagBucks.

Sell Websites

Did you know that you can make money buying and selling websites? Well now you know. There is an abundance of websites on a multitude of topics that can pop up in your head. It's not over yet. These websites also make a lot of money through ads, affiliates, products and memberships. Furthermore, these websites are also sometimes put on sale, which provides buyers like you to purchase them. A great online platform for buying and selling websites is Exchange Marketplace. On this platform, you can buy and sell ecommerce stores.

Moreover, once you sign up, the process is 100% secure, and you don't have to worry about privacy violations or any infringements. This approach also helps save time and money. All you have to do is to manage and run a store that is already making a sufficient amount of money. On top of that, once you have purchased a website, you will also receive seller support to ensure you get a hang of how things are done on that specific website.

Sell Your Designs Online

The Internet is a marketplace that can help you sell anything in time, and at a good price. Designs aren't an exception, when we talk about things to sell online. Just like other platforms we have discussed so far, there are some platforms aimed specifically at selling designs. Some great examples are ThemeForest, 99Designs and the Creative Market.

Whether you sell templates, illustrations, branding resources or fonts, these online platforms have got you covered. You might not know this yet, but the design industry in the US is worth a staggering $13.11 billion. If you are good at what you do and if you remain persistent, you can get a bigger piece of the pie.

If you want to sell your designs on the creative market, you won't have to wait for approval before you can think about making some money. On the flipside, when you do it online, there are no such strings attached. Moreover, the online route allows you your own personal storefront to take your business forward.

Start Selling NFTs

While there is an entire chapter aimed specifically at NFTs, consider this an overview. Chances are you are new to the ideas of NFTs. Well, NFTs or non-fungible tokens are digital assets that are stored on a digital ledger. The great thing about NFTs is that the assets that you store over a digital ledger can be more valuable than you can even imagine.

Moreover, there are endless possibilities when it comes to non-fungible tokens. You can make NFTs for digital designs, music, art pieces, games, GIFs and even videos. Furthermore, creating an NFT that will sell is easier than most people think. You can use platforms like OpenSea and follow the step by step minting process which is easy and self-explanatory.

While NFTs are something new, the NFT market has already gone past the $10 million mark. This is the perfect time to enter the fold and benefit from the profitability these NFTs can offer. However, you must remember that you need some upfront investment to get in, but your investment is nothing compared to the values NFTs can offer.

Make Job Boards

Job boards are an easy yet effective means to make some passive income as an online entrepreneur. These websites are stashed all across the internet, and they are used by employers to share job vacancies and attract the right talent. These websites serve as a bridge between the employers and the potential job seekers. You can have your own job board where employers can advertise their job vacancies.

In return, you can charge these employers a small sum of money which is not too heavy on their wallet, while it helps you make a decent amount over time. With time, you can also offer premium features like unlimited access to candidate base or sponsored jobs. You may not have the resources or the time to build a job board from scratch. It's alright if you don't. You can always purchase a readymade template online, and start a job board of your own.

While it is easy to start out with a job board, marketing it the right way is what needs some genuine work, but before you back off, please read on. While there is no magic pill, all you have to do is to stay persistent. Investing in social media and SEO is profitable, but try your best to retain your customers so they return to you, while recommending your job board to others. If you lack inspiration, you can check out platforms like Dribble, ProBlogger, and Construction Jobs.

No-Code Applications

You may consider it rocket science, but creating a beginner to advanced level application is actually possible for any novice, if they use no-code tools. If you don't have much information on how applications are made, you can try out tools like Appy Pie, Bubble or Adalo.

These tools can allow you to make your own applications that serve various purposes and contribute to the industry that had a record number of 218 billion downloads in 2020 only. Just imagine how high that number would have touched during the past two years. To begin with, you will have to decide whether or not you have to design a mobile application or a website.

Next up, you will have to think about the niche it will serve. You will also have to think about monetization, because that is where a large percentage of your money will come from. Monetization can happen in a number of ways including ads, subscriptions, and pay to downloads.

Ear Royalties for Inventions

If you think inventors are a thing of the past, it might also be the reason why you have struggled to make some passive income. Well, your perspective is about to change. You can be an inventor, and one that earns royalty for their inventions. The hardest part of an inventor's journey is getting started, but the payout is worth the struggle and the hard work that you put in.

Before you begin, it is worth noting that your invention must be aimed at solving a specific problem or a number of problems, or else it won't sell. To be on the safe side, visit the US Patent website, as it will give you an idea of whether or not your idea has been used before. If it hasn't been used by anyone else, you can be the first one. If you have already come up with a unique product, you can resort to online platforms like Invention City or Invent My Idea. Depending upon what deal you strike, you can start making a decent amount of money in royalties.

Minimizing Taxes on Passive Income Streams

A passive income stream is a great side hustle. However, with these passive income streams come tax liabilities. There are ways to minimize your taxes, though. You can set yourself up as a business, or you can create a retirement account. It is worth noting that this strategy won't apply to all passive income strategies. Here is what you need to do.

- First of all, you have to register with the IRS, and you will receive a tax identification number for the business.
- Next up you can get in touch with a broker to open up a self-employed account for your retirement.
- You also have to determine the kind of retirement account that is most suitable for you.

Two of the most popular options in this regard are the SEP IRA and the solo 401(k). If you put your cash in either of the two accounts, you can enjoy some tax breaks on your annual taxes. The great thing about the 401(k) is that you can stuff all of your earnings into that account up to the annual maximum. On the flip side, the SEP IRA only allows a 25% contribution. Moreover, the 401(k) allows you to contribute 25% of your annual profits as well.

Myths about Passive Income

The idea of passive income is very attractive, especially when you need to make some extra money. Furthermore, for some strange reason, the idea of making money in a passive fashion seems easier than working a 9-5 job. Probably, it is due to the picture painted by the much celebrated business tycoons making thousands of dollars a second. We humans are impressionable, and no matter how much we resist, we fall prey to the passive income myths that are sold to us on a daily basis. While it is possible to make money from a side hustle, not everything we hear is true. In this section, I will bust some myths about passive income, and provide you with some clarity.

You Can Set Your Revenue Streams and Forget About Them

This is the biggest lie that we often hear about passive income. This is how humans are wired. We automatically entertain any idea of making money without having to move a muscle, but unfortunately, that isn't the way the world functions. Let's suppose you run a blog or an online store as a side hustle. Do you think it will help you generate money without putting in new content, or without showcasing new products? The answer is no. The people subscribing to your blog demand fresh content or else they are meant to bounce. Moreover, the internet itself is evolving by the minute, and the only way to stay relevant is to put out new stuff on a regular basis.

If you don't put in the hard yards and don't put out sufficient content, your followers will go to someone that does. Consequently, your passive income stream will dry up in no time, and the hardest part will be to get your business back on its feet once again. Let's suppose you have hired a couple of people to handle your side business for you. Do you really think you can delegate responsibilities, not follow up, and expect your business to deliver the results? You will have to revisit your gig from time to time, in order for it to yield the results for which you initially set it up in the first place.

You Only Need a Weekend to Get Started

Sure enough, most passive income streams don't require a phenomenal amount of money or time, but it doesn't mean things will happen overnight. I'm sorry to bust this myth for you, but before you earn a single penny, you will have to carry out considerable research, and chances are you might even fail during the first few attempts before you can get it right. You might think that setting up a blog, or investing in a startup will make you money right away, you need to get your facts straight.

Starting a blog might seem simple, but in order to start, you will have to choose a niche, and also figure out whether or not there is sufficient audience out there that will follow your blog. You can't write about a topic that isn't popular and expect the idea to be a success. That story also doesn't end with you choosing the right topic to write about. Even if your content is relevant, and is appealing to the masses, you will have to market it so it reaches the final consumer. You will still have to deploy digital techniques like search engine optimization, which don't come cheap, and also require sufficient digital expertise. Moreover, you will also have to incorporate all the necessary images and video elements to your content for it to be comprehensive.

With so much to do, do you think you'll be able to pull off over the weekend? Remember, generating passive income isn't a race that you have to win. It is something that requires perseverance, and it takes a lot of trial and error before you can get it right.

All You Need Is a Solid Income Source

This is partially true, but how can you make something earn you money if you don't know what to make of it. Even if you do, you need multiple passive streams to be able to generate sufficient money. With this approach, you will have all of your stock market investments in a single company. If the stocks do well, you will be successful, but if they fail, the results at your end will be disastrous.

Now that we are on the topic of stocks, let's talk about it. When dealing in stocks, it is better to diversify your approach rather than investing in something singular, especially when you are searching for something to replace your salary.

Let's go back to the example of online blogging. There are some bloggers out there that receive lesser web traffic. Therefore, they can't rely solely on their blog to make money for them. They have to complement their blogging efforts by using affiliate links, by providing online courses, and also by offering online services. By increasing your passive income streams, it will be easier for you to earn enough to be able to support your plans.

Real Estate Is 100% Safe

Real estate is an effective passive income stream, but to call it the safest is just not right. With the prices of real estate hiking throughout the country, most people are beginning to invest in this passive income stream, which can be profitable in some cases, but this technique can also backfire.

This might be new for you, but realistic property management is never fully passive. In fact, there are certain costs involved with real estate. These costs include repairs and the day to day expenses of maintaining a piece of property. Sometimes, these costs are so much that they eat up all of your chances of making money from the piece of real estate you own. You might even have to deal with bad tenants, which can consume a significant portion of your time, not to mention the stress that comes with it.

A few weeks into property management, your perspective will change. The reason is that real estate doesn't offer the ROI that you expect it to provide. Moreover, studies have shown that one out of three property managers say that they won't invest in the same piece of property ever again. While managing a property can indeed work out in your favor, selling a property after its value increases is always a better option than holding on to it for an extended period of time. The increasing number of costs involved with property management will only put you under more financial stress.

You Need a Solid Business Idea

Whenever a group of people with little or no knowledge of passive income communicates, the only thing they talk about is the importance of buying property, and how you need a business idea. But unfortunately, this isn't always the case. Some people even generate passive income by putting money in retirement accounts, as well as savings accounts. While the latter approach isn't always as lucrative as having a big idea, it surely offers a risk-free way of arranging money for fulfilling one's financial plans.

According to most investors, you can only earn a return of 5% per annum. This may not seem much, but in the long run, the return can accumulate into something substantial, thus benefiting you financially, and taking care of your needs. On the flipside, even if you have a solid business idea, the right entrepreneurial skills to make it come to life, and the resources to back it up, a business can still fail, thus sending all of your investments down the drain. Instead, it is better to take a less lucrative approach that is safe, and doesn't present you with risks that are substantial in nature. I don't mean that you must not take risks, but you must only take them when you have the means to handle a failure.

You Need a Lot of Money to Earn Passive Income

One of the most common misconceptions that exist among a lot of people is that in order to make passive income, you need a lot of money. While money is important, this isn't always the case. If you plan on investing in stocks, you can do so with as little as $1000. In the case of blogging, you can get web hosting for not more than $8 a month.

It is a fact that putting your additional savings towards powering your business idea or online blog is beneficial to your ideas. However, what truly matters is whether or not you are willing to research the current state of the market, as well as the opportunities and risks attached to your investment. Furthermore, carrying out the right background checks will help you utilize your financial resources as wisely as possible, while ensuring the profitability that you are looking for. While money can make the world go round, with a little creativity, you can do great things with a minimal amount, only if you plan your cards right, and harp on all possible opportunities while avoiding the risks and challenges.

Chapter 5: Tips and Tricks to Manage Debt

It is very difficult to accomplish your financial goals when you have to pay your debts. The truth about debt is that it is like a spiral that never comes to an end. If you are looking for ways to control your debt, you are already halfway there to solving your problem.

Before you move forward, please remember that debt isn't always a bad thing. Take a mortgage, for example. It helps you own property and have a place you can call home. Furthermore, you can become wealthy when your property appreciates in value. However, most debt is not positive, and in this chapter, we will look at some effective ways to manage debt.

Bump Up the Debt Repayment Rate

Most credit card companies ask you to pay almost 2 percent of the outstanding balance every month. Therefore, you can use at least 15% of your money from your salaries and social security/pensions to pay your credit card debt. By doing so, you will find it easier to pay off this liability quickly. Making small payments each month will take longer for you to pay your credit card debt. Therefore, it is better to make larger payments and get done with your credit card debt to be able to focus on other things.

Use Your Savings to Pay Your Debts

Saving can also come in handy when trying to pay off debts. The smart thing to do is to utilize cash reserves for debt payments. This way, you won't have to accrue interest on larger balances. Sure, it is very comforting to have some extra cash in your bank account, but the truth is, those funds aren't completely working for you.

At least not with the low interest rates of today. You don't have to deplete all of your savings. If you have a large sum of cash, you might as well use some of it to pay off debts. By doing so, you will make your payments on time, and you won't even have to take out large amounts of cash to do so.

Negotiate a Lower Interest Rate

A great way to manage your debt is to talk to your creditors and negotiate a lower interest rate on your debt. If you have a good credit history and account standing, you will be amazed at how easy it is for creditors to offer you a lower interest rate. Moreover, if you have always paid your debts on time and maintained a good relationship with your creditors, they will show you some leniency, and offer a lower rate of interest. With lesser interest payments, you will save some money when you pay your liability during the course of a year.

Use a Tax Refund Check

When you have some extra money on you, it can be tempting enough for you to splurge on some luxury items or to go for a vacation with your friends and family. If you act smartly, you can use your money to pay off debt. The most annoying thing about debts is the monthly payments you have to make. Wouldn't it be amazing to make a hefty payment, only to lessen the burden of debt?

With a tax refund check, you can make a sufficient payment on your liability, which keeps you from being too overwhelmed with large monthly payments throughout the year. Think about it. Would you prefer spending money on something so perishable when you can really pay off some debt? Of course, you'd choose the latter. At least I would.

Make Cash Sales

Selling items for cash is another great way to pay off debt. The internet should be your go-to medium for making sales. To begin with, make a list of things that you don't need anymore. It could be a used car, an electrical appliance, a computer, a mobile phone, or a piece of furniture. Once you have listed all of those things, you can sell them on eBay and Craigslist. You can even sell at a garage sale. The proceeds that come from your sale can be used to pay off debt, thus helping you save your hard-earned cash and spending them on products and services you genuinely need, or you can also save up for your retirement.

Cash Your Life Insurance

Utilizing your life insurance is a great strategy for paying off debt. It allows you to pay off larger chunks of debt quicker than you would otherwise pay. Paying debt from your life insurance is also a great way to get some relief if you are drowning in debt. It becomes even easier when you don't have any beneficiaries, such as a spouse or children.

However, such a strategy doesn't apply if you have a term life insurance policy. It only applies to whole life insurance policies that have a built-up cash value. It is also worth noting that even if you have beneficiaries, you can still use a part of the built-up value of your whole life insurance policy for debt reduction while leaving some value for your loved ones.

Make Extra Money

If you plan on paying off all of your debt within the same year, you are already on the right path. However, to pay off your debt, it is important for you to make some extra money, to be able to pay it off quickly. There are several ways you can do so.

You can either invest in a side business or build up a few passive income streams. You can also uplift your performance at work, thus bagging valuable appraisals and paying off debt with all of that extra money.

Balance Transfers on Credit Card

The credit card balances that end up in our mailboxes are often torn up. However, if you want to minimize your debts, balance transfers can surely come in handy. It is even possible for you to eliminate all of your credit card interest. All you have to do is to transfer all of your high rate debt to a zero percent deal; a deal that lasts for a year or so. By doing so, you can free up your cash flow, which allows you to pay credit card bills. However, before you sign any paperwork, make sure you have read the fine print to know what you are getting.

Statute of Limitations

Interestingly, some people tend to pay off really old credit card debts, even though there is no legal obligation for them to do so. However, if times are financially tough for you, it is better to pay off current debts rather than the ones that are 7-10 years old.

When it comes to outstanding debt, each state has its own rules and regulations. Some states don't allow debt collectors to collect a specific kind of debt after a specific period of time.

Other states can minimize the amount of time for debt payment if the collector has the option to sue you for not paying off the debt. Irrespective of the scenario, it is better for you to figure out whether or not the limitation statute has passed on an old one that you may owe. If it has passed, your problems are over. You can freely forgo repayment without worrying about any legal or financial issues.

Dealing with old debts can be confusing. However, you should contact your state attorney general or the consumer protection agency. They will help you better understand the statute of limitations and the complexities surrounding outstanding debt.

File for Bankruptcy

The reason why filing bankruptcy has the last spot on this list is that it only always be used as a last resort to get rid of debt. However, when you don't have any cash on you, and you have to pay medical bills or credit card bills, it is always appropriate for you to file for bankruptcy.

Things to Consider Before Taking Out a Personal Loan

There are multiple benefits of personal loans. First of all, they help avoid credit cards, and secondly, they help you finance big purchases, without having to pay a hefty amount of interest.

Lending Tree is one of the most popular online lending platforms in the US. According to one of their researches, personal loans are becoming increasingly popular, with more than 20.2 million personal borrowers in the country.

Whether you take out a loan to consolidate your debt, to make improvements to your home, or to plan a trip with friends and family, it is important to have a repayment plan. If you are planning to take out a personal loan, here are a few things you need to factor in.

How Much Do You Need

Before taking out a personal loan, you need to be very specific about the amount of money you need. While the minimum personal limit is $500, most lenders lend not less than $1000 or $2000. If you need $500 or less, you can borrow the amount from a friend or a family member. This will make it easier for you to save some extra money in advance. If you want a smaller loan, you can reach out to unions like PenFed. PenFed is a credit union that offers a variety of small loan options. With PenFed, you can borrow as little as $600 which can range up to $50,000.

Should You Pay Your Creditors Directly

In the case of a personal loan, the cash is usually delivered to a checking account. However, if you take out a personal loan for the purpose of debt consolidation, things can change a bit.

There are some lenders out there that allow you to send cash directly to them, without having to use your bank account.

On the flipside, if you prefer a hands-on approach, or if you don't want to use a personal loan to existing debt, it is better to connect your payment process to your checking account. You can also opt for a no-fee personal loan for debt consolidation purposes. A great example in this regard is a personal loan by Marcus by Goldman Sachs. These personal loans don't need the borrowers to pay a fee for personal loans. With the Marcus personal loan, the borrower is allowed to send money to almost 10 creditors, while any additional money is deposited directly into the linked bank account.

How Long Will You Take to Pay

The time you need to repay your creditor is also an important thing to consider. Usually, the monthly installment process takes off only a month after you borrow the money. Depending upon your lender, the repayment duration can range between six months and a few years. The length of your loan will impact the monthly payments, as well as the interest you pay. Let's suppose, the repayment duration is anywhere between three to seven years. The increase in duration will minimize your monthly payments.

However, you will end up paying extra money in interest. By paying the interest, not only will you compensate your lender for the time you take, but it will also enable you to keep your credit report intact. On the flipside, if the duration of your debt is short, it will increase your monthly payments, but it will also save you from higher interest. Regardless of your loan duration, it is better to pay more each month. First of all, it allows you to pay your loan quickly, while not having to pay extra money in interest.

How Much Will You Pay in Interest

The interest rate that we discussed in the previous paragraph depends upon a number of different factors. These factors include the loan amount, the term of your loan, and your credit score. Your interest rate can be anywhere between 3.5% and 29.9%. As we have already discussed, if you have a good credit score, and you opt for a shorter loan term, you can end up with a lower interest rate.

According to some recent data by the Fed, the average APR for a 2-year personal loan is a little over nine percent. This interest rate is much lower than an average APR on a credit card. This is also one of the reasons why a lot of people take out personal loans to pay off their credit card debt. Moreover, a personal loan is fixed, and it remains the same throughout the life of your loan.

Can You Really Afford the Monthly Payment

This may seem trivial, but before you take out a personal loan, it is important for you to factor in whether or not you can afford your monthly payments. You need to make sure whether or not your monthly income and your monthly cash flow can handle the extent of your payments, so it is better to choose your repayment plan accordingly. If you resort to autopay, some lenders might give you an incentive. In most cases, they end up lowering your APR by 0.25 to 0.50%.

Some people choose to make low monthly payments. As a result, they end up for months and years at a stretch. Others choose to make high monthly payments, which helps them pay off the entire amount in a short amount of time. As discussed earlier, choosing to make minimum payments comes at the cost of paying a higher amount of interest. As a result, the borrower ends up paying much more than the amount of their loan.

Usually, what happens is that a borrower doesn't spend more than 35-40% of their monthly pay on debt payments. For better understanding, look at it this way. Let's suppose your monthly income is $4000. If such is the case, your monthly payment might amount to $1700 or a little over that.

It is worth noting that most mortgage lenders refuse to lend money to borrowers with a debt-to-income ratio of more than 43%. On the flipside, most personal loan lenders tend to be more lenient with their approach. However, in order to benefit from their forgiving nature, it is important to have a good credit score, and a proven source of income. It is also possible to stretch the debt-to-income ratio. All you have to do is to prove that you can handle higher monthly payments. By doing so, you will stretch this ratio, and also save money that would otherwise be spent on interest payments.

One must remember that stretching your debt-to-income ratio is not as easy as one thinks. Even if you somehow manage to do so, it can result in some major cash flow problems down the line. This measure is risky, and therefore it should only be adopted temporarily, unless you are backed by some kind of partner's income or an emergency fund.

Do Personal Loans Have Any Fees

This answer is yes. Personal loan lenders charge some sign-up fees or origination fees. However, most of them don't charge anything else except the interest rate that we just mentioned. If you don't know already, an origination cost is the amount of money subtracted from the lent amount to pay the processing fees, and the administration charges. An origination fee is somewhere between 1% and 5% of the original amount. However, some lenders have a flat-rate origination fee. For example, some of them would charge 5% regardless of how much you are borrowing. For example, if your personal loan amounts to $10,000, you won't get more than $9500. It is best to avoid these fees, as much as possible.

Is Your Credit Score Good Enough

That's right, your credit score is more crucial to the loan process than you think. It affects the borrowed amount, the length of your loan, your monthly payments, as well as the interest rate you end up paying. Most lenders take the borrower's credit score very seriously. Usually online banks are very particular about the credit score. However, things become a lot easier if you have been associated with a bank for a longer period of time, and you have made your bill payments on time, while honoring the terms and conditions used by your bank.

If a borrower has a decent credit score, their credit union will end up lowering their interest rates on the borrowed personal loans. But there are some strings attached. In some cases, you will have to be a member of the credit union, and in some cases, you might even need to have opened a personal account.

But you shouldn't feel too discouraged if your current credit score is not up to par. With avenues like UPSTART, applicants with less than satisfactory credit score can also get approved. However, it is most likely that you will end up paying more money and fees compared to what you would have to pay, if you had a good credit score. For your own safety, it is advised to read the terms and conditions of the loan very carefully.

What Other Choices Do You Have

If you are looking for ways to pay off debt, a balance transfer card can come in handy. The best thing about these cards is that they help you save money on interest. These cards come with a promotional 0% APR, which stays the same for as long as 21 months, thus helping you save hundreds of dollars.

Moreover, depending upon your situation, you also have the option to transfer your credit card balance to another card. However, the total must not exceed your credit limit. Some of the best options at your disposal are Citi Simplicity Card, the Fargo Reflect Card and the US Bank Platinum Visa Card.

However, there are some downsides to the balance transfer cards, such as balance transfer fees, and balance transfer limits. The limits are actually lesser than your actual credit card. Moreover, you will have to pay the fees, unless you opt for a no-fee alternative such as the Wings Visa Platinum Card. Other than offering a 0% fee, these cards help you make large purchases that you wish to pay off over time.

How Soon Are the Funds Needed

One thing you need to ask yourself before seeking a personal loan is when the amount is needed. There are some money lending options that pay the same day your loan is approved. A great example of such lenders is Lightstream. With Lightstream you don't have to wait at all. Then some lenders such as

Discover Personal Loans take one business day, transferring funds the next day. Then there are those that can take as much as 10 business days. If you are in dire need of money, it is better to opt for lending platforms like Lightstream.

Will It Impact Your Credit Score

You might not know, but personal loans fall within the category of installment credit, while credit cards fall in the category of revolving credit. Having both the credit types on your portfolio will help strengthen your credit situation. While credit diversity is important, it is not the only thing you need, in order to strengthen your credit score. Some people say that taking out an auto loan will help improve your credit score, but it is pointless to take out a loan for something you don't need.

While other things may play a part in enhancing your credit score, there are two things you need to focus on. First, try to make timely payments, and secondly, focus on credit utilization. You must remember that taking on an installment loan won't improve your credit score. However, using a personal loan to pay off a revolving debt will allow you to increase your credit score significantly. Once you pay off your credit card, keep spending less than 10% of your remaining credit and keep tabs on your credit score. Luckily, there are widgets out there that help you find loan offers. The great thing about this option is that it helps you land a personal loan without hurting your credit score.

Chapter 6: Ways to Avoid Debt

Financial health and debt can rarely work together, and in most cases, debt has the ability to damage you financially. However, your debt doesn't necessarily have to be your enemy.

For example, if you're looking for a loan to pay your college fees, and you have a strong plan to pay off that debt on time, you can build a good credit history. This allows you to get better financing in the future while achieving your personal, professional, or financial goals.

However, in some cases, it is in your best interest to avoid debt as much as possible. A common example is credit card debt. When you pay a minimal amount towards the end of every month, you end up with heaps of interest to pay, which can be overwhelming for you, especially if you have a shortage of funds or a limited cash flow at your end.

Another example is that of a car loan. A car loan can stretch up your budget, thus making you financially uncomfortable. As a result, you can fall behind in your payments, and it can also keep you from making more important payments such as utility bills.

Here are some easy but effective ways to avoid debt altogether.

Building an Emergency Fund

It may sound a little weird, but saving in an emergency fund can be helpful in avoiding debt. According to some experts, it is better to save almost three to six months of expenses, and even more if your work is seasonal in nature or unpredictable, to be more specific. By doing so, you will provide your savings a cushion, even if you go bankrupt or lose a job.

Another great thing about an emergency fund is that it saves important expenses that would otherwise end up on your credit card. If your car is in need of some urgent repairs or you need to go see a doctor, you can easily utilize your emergency fund to pay for it. As a result, you won't have to resort to your credit card at all, which will save you from some long-term debt.

Choose Your Spending Plans

Things can become really difficult for you if you are making purchases on your credit card and you are unable to pay on time. The amount continues to pile up, thus overwhelming you. The smartest way to avoid debt in this scenario is to have a solid plan for each dollar you earn.

When you make a budget, it is better to divide it into needs and wants, as well as long-term and short-term financial goals, with a 50/30/20 plan. A zero-based budget adds perspective to every dollar, so at least you know where your money is going. Regardless of which strategy you opt for, it becomes easier for you to track expenses, thus making sure that you are spending less than what you earn.

Follow a Savings Routine

By automating your savings strategy, you can make your life easier. A savings routine can help you put aside money for your retirement plans, as well as an emergency fund. Furthermore, when that money is separated from your checking account, it becomes easier for you not to spend it and go into any kind of debt. If you don't pay directly from your paycheck, you can easily automate your monthly transfers into your retirement fund or emergency fund.

Ways to Get Out of Debt

Up until now, we have discussed some of the ways to avoid debt, but what will you do when you are already struggling with debt, and you want to get out of it? In the previous chapter, I spoke of ways to minimize debt, but these tips will help you set yourself free from any debt problem, for that matter.

Reexamine the Budget

The two simplest ways to get rid of debt is to make more money and spend much less than what you have. While some people lack the time to work a part-time job, others lack the resources and the entrepreneurial skills to start a side hustle. However, no matter which category you fall into, you can always make some adjustments to your budget. What you need to do is to revisit your spending plans. Look at each item in that plan, and sort those items according to their level of importance. Figure out whether an item is a necessity or a want. Look at all the expenses and ask yourself whether they are important enough to secure a spot on your spending plan. If they can be eliminated, do so right away. If you can't eliminate those expenses altogether, you can always try to minimize them. The money you save will help you eventually pay off your debt and get out of it once and for all.

Pay More than the Minimum Level of Payment

Look at your budget and your debt. Now, try to figure out how much extra money you can afford to put in. If you can, then do so. This approach is good for two reasons. First of all, it helps you pay a lower interest rate, and secondly, it allows you to get out of debt as quickly as possible, depending on your debt payments. Let's suppose you are dealing with credit card debt, and you have an APR that is 17%, while your minimum payment is $450. If you don't think creatively, you will end up paying the bare minimum, and it will take you a couple of years before you can get rid of your debt. Moreover, you will also pay more than $5000 in nothing but pure interest. On the flip side, if you pay a sum of $550 or $100 more than your minimum payment, you will easily get rid of your debt in less than three years. Moreover, you will also be paying just a little over $4000 in interest.

Resort to the Debt Snowball

If you are paying more than the minimum monthly payment, you must give yourself a pat on the back, for you are on the right path. The good news is, you can also try the debt snowball method, but what is it anyway? Well, the debt snowball method requires a person to make minimum payments on all of their debts, except for the smallest ones. As the name implies, the person in debt snowballs payments toward their smallest debts until it is completely eliminated before moving to the next smallest debt.

Let's suppose you have a credit card balance amounting to $6000, an auto loan of $2000, and a student loan amounting to $12000. If you follow the snowball approach, you will try to get rid of the auto loan because it is the smallest and the easiest to pay off. You will then move to the credit card and eventually student loan.

With the snowball method, you get to focus on one debt at a time before moving to the next. First of all, it keeps you from being too overwhelmed, and secondly, it helps you stay on track. The only time you should avoid the snowball method is when there is a payday loan or a title loan. The reason is, these loans tend to have a much higher APR which ranges between 300-500%.

Refinance Your Debt

Refinancing your debt is helpful for two reasons. First up, it helps you save money that you would otherwise spend on interest. Secondly, it helps you pay your debt much faster. Moreover, whether it is an auto loan, personal loan, student loan, or a mortgage, all of them can be refinanced. There are a number of ways to refinance your debt. Your first option is to opt for a Debt Consolidation Loan.

It is a kind of personal loan with an interest rate that is lower than that on your existing debts. If your debt is because of a credit card, one suitable option is to transfer it to a Balance Transfer Card. The great thing about the Balance Transfer Cars is that it offers a 0% APR for a specific amount of time, which is somewhere between six and 18 months.

Commit Windfalls

Sometimes you can get a stimulus check or a tax refund. With all of that extra money, you can easily pay your debt, or at least a percentage of it. It is very tempting to save all of that money in a savings account or splurge on luxuries, but it is better to be smart about it, and use that money to pay your debts. Now, it is up to you whether you choose to commit the entire windfall to debt payment or split it 50-50, splurging the other 50% on something fun. Some other possible windfalls include bonuses, inheritances, and cash gifts. You must remember that each payment is important; as it helps you move a step closer to paying your debt.

Types of Debt

We have already talked so much about debt prevention. Let's shift gear just a little bit and talk about some of the most common types of debts that you might face at some point in your life.

Secured Debt

A secured debt is the one for which collateral is put up. Two common examples of secured loans are auto loans and mortgages. In the case of an auto loan, a vehicle is used as collateral, while mortgages use a piece of real estate as a form of collateral. In the event that you fail to pay a secured debt, the debt can be seized by the lender, which results in a foreclosure on your property, or a repossession in the case of an auto loan.

There are times when the seized collateral doesn't suffice. If that happens, the creditor might take you to the court of law in order to recover the remaining amount. For example, if your auto loan amounts to $10,000 and your vehicle can only provide $7000, you will have to pay the remaining $3000 from your own wallet.

There are other forms of secured debt which include a home equity line of credit and a home equity loan. In either case, your home will serve as collateral to secure the debt.

Let's look at some of the benefits of secured debts.

- First of all, it allows you to borrow a large amount of money, for the creditor is absolutely certain that they will get their money back, regardless. They will seize your property or your vehicle, or they will take you to court.
- Because a secured debt presents the lender with a lesser amount of risk, and they know they'll get their money back, the borrower is not bound to pay a higher interest rate.
- The best part about a secured debt is that it offers you tax deductions based on the interest paid on an auto loan or a mortgage.

Now, let's talk about the disadvantages of secured debt.

- First up, your inability to pay the loan back can make you lose your property or your vehicle while having to pay the remaining amount.
- Secondly, with secured debt, you borrow money for a specific purpose, and you can only use that money for

the purpose for which it is intended. You cannot use it for other expenses or repayment of other debts.

Now, let's look at some ways to handle a secured debt.

- Make sure to make your payments on time, and while it is better to pay some extra money, at least pay the minimum monthly amount.
- If you are having a hard time making payments, make sure to let your lender know in the beginning. If you let them know right in the start, chances are they will simplify the payment plan for you.
- If it is almost impossible for you to pay the lender, it is better to sell the property. Selling your car or your property will allow you to repay the debt without having to go to court, which is also a possibility. Moreover, by doing so, you will keep your credit report from any possible blemishes.

Unsecured Debt

Unlike secured debt, unsecured debt is one that isn't backed by a specific asset. Instead, it is the amount you borrow purely because of your creditworthiness or your ability to pay it back. Here are some of the most common examples of unsecured debts.

- Student loans

- Personal loans
- Credit cards
- Medical bills

As we know, in the case of unsecured debts, a creditor cannot seize your property or your car. However, if you fail to make your payments on time, the creditor can report your case to the top credit bureaus, thus putting you in a lot of trouble. The creditor can also approach a debt collector and even go to court.

Let's look at some of the benefits of an unsecured loan.

- To begin with, you don't have to own property in order to get hold of a student loan or a credit card.
- Your debt isn't backed by collateral that your lender can seize.
- Lastly, your request to secure an unsecured loan can be approved much quicker than you think.

Now, let's look at some of the demerits of an unsecured loan.

- Unlike secured debt, unsecured debt can present you with a higher interest rate. When it comes to extending an unsecured loan, the lender takes a significant amount of risk, which results in a higher interest rate.

- Unless you have a decent credit history, you will find it much more difficult to secure such a loan.

Here are some easy ways to handle an unsecured loan.

- Make sure to make the minimum possible payments and that too on time.
- If you lag behind in terms of payments, make sure to reach out to your creditor before they come to you. Share your problems with them, and nine times out of ten, they will help you with a payment plan.

Revolving Debt

It sounds weird, but a revolving debt can either be a secured debt or an unsecured one. A credit card is the perfect example of unsecured revolving debt. On the flip side, a home equity line of credit is a secured revolving debt. Simply put, a revolving account is the one that has a specific credit limit that the lender sets.

The available credit continues to decrease with each purchase, and it increases with each payment. Moreover, the balance amount dictates the fluctuation in the minimum amount due. Let's look at some of the best ways to handle a revolving debt.

- Be very careful about your spending.

- Make full payment each month. If you are unable to do so, try to pay a bit more than the bare minimum. Also, try your best to make your payments before the due date.
- If you are having a hard time making payments, make sure to pay the high-interest debts before paying for the low-interest ones. This is known as the debt avalanche method. It helps you pay a lower interest rate as the time passes.

Installment Debt

Before confusion gets to you, remember that an installment isn't any different from a non-revolving debt. In the case of an installment, the borrower gets a lump sum amount of money, which can be used for the consolidation for existing debts. Let's suppose you are a borrower and you get a loan amounting to $10,000. Each month, you will have to pay an installment of $300. This payment plan will have to be completed within a period of three years, i.e. 36 months. Like revolving debts, an installment debt can be secured or unsecured. Some of the common examples of installments are as follows.

- Personal loans
- Auto loans
- Student loans

- Mortgages

Let's check out some of the most effective ways to handle an installment debt.

- Always pay on time, and make full payments.
- Try to make your payments on a weekly basis, rather than doing it month by month. First of all, it will help you pay off your debt quickly, and secondly, it will help you avoid a higher interest rate.
- Even if you stick to monthly payments, try to shell out a few bucks more than the minimum monthly payment. For example, if you make a monthly payment of $150, try expanding it to $200, to be able to pay off the debt quickly.
- If it is hard for you to pay extra money each month, or to make weekly payments, try to make one extra payment each year. This approach will decrease the loan duration, while preventing a higher interest rate.
- You can also refinance the loan, as it allows you to pay it off quickly, and also avoid high interest rates.

Can't Pay off Debt? Try Debt Relief

Sometimes it becomes difficult for a borrower to pay off the loan. It gets even worse when the lenders are up for revising the existing payment plan. If you are in such a situation right now, you can resort to debt relief. There are two ways to do so. Either you can consult a credit counseling agency, or seek help from a company that provides debt relief. The great thing about credit counseling agencies is that they help you come up with a budget that further helps you pay off debt, while providing you with other solutions to handle your debt better. Some of these solutions are as follows.

Debt Management

One such solution is a debt management plan. In the case of debt management, your credit counseling agency works with unsecured creditors to work a payment plan for you. These creditors can help you in a number of ways. For example, they can either reduce your interest rate or waive off certain fees. With debt management, you make payments to your credit counseling agency, which divides that money among the unsecured lenders.

Debt Settlement

Another way to deal with heaps of unsecured debts is resorting to a debt settlement program. Although this alternative is effective, it is risky, and is costly. Therefore, it must always be used as the last resort, if all else fails. What happens typically is that the company negotiates your payment plan with your creditors.

As a result, you have to pay a lump sum amount which is slightly lesser than what you originally owe. To make a lump sum payment, you start to put aside a small sum of money each month. This money continues to accumulate in that account until there is enough for you to make the lump sum payment, and get rid of your debt once and for all.

However, it is worth noting that not making regular payments can have a bad impact upon your credit report, which can cause problems further down the line. Moreover, in the case of lump sum payments the lenders also charge fees for the delay in payments, which can come off as an added financial burden.

Refinancing

In the previous paragraphs, we shared with you the idea of refinancing a loan. In this section, we will delve deeper into the definition of refinancing, how it works, and what are some of the pros and cons of refinancing a debt. Let's dive in.

As the name implies, refinancing a loan is the process of revising the terms on which a credit agreement is based. When a person or a business refinances a loan, they make certain changes to the interest rate, the payment schedule and the additional terms and conditions applied to the credit agreement. If the refinance request is approved by the lender, the new contract replaces the original contract, and all the payments are made accordingly.

Individuals and organizations usually opt for a refinance when the interest rate hikes drastically. It allows them to save a sufficient amount of money that would otherwise be spent on paying interest.

How it works

Most borrowers opt for loan refinance when there is an aggressive shift within the economic conditions. It helps them obtain borrowing terms that are more favorable. Here are some of the most common goals behind opting for a refinance.

- It helps revise the interest rates.
- It helps revise the payment schedules and duration of the loan.
- It also helps the borrowers to move from a fixed rate mortgage to an adjustable rate mortgage.

Some borrowers also refinance a loan when their economic conditions or their credit conditions improve. A refinance can also allow them to consolidate their loan into one lump sum payment that won't damage their credit standing. Because the new consolidated loan is lower than the original amount, it won't come off as an added burden to the wallet.

As we have already discussed, the most common reason for people to refinance is due to the changes in the interest rates that are cyclical in nature. This is part of the reason so many people choose to refinance when there is a drop in interest rates. But what causes a fluctuation in the interest rates? There are several reasons such as the national monetary policy, the market completion, and the economic cycles. These factors can impact all kinds of credit products, whether they are revolving or non-revolving in nature. When there is a hike in interest rates, the debtors with variable rates end up paying more, and vice versa.

It is also worth mentioning that in order to refinance their loans; a debtor can either approach their current creditor or a new one, while requesting them to approve the new loan request. As a result, refinancing involves the reevaluation of the borrowers' financial situation and credit terms. The most common types of loans that are refinanced include student loans, car loans and mortgages.

It's not only the individual borrowers that refinance loans. Businesses also opt for refinancing in order to deal with debt. It usually happens in the case of commercial properties. A lot of business investors tend to evaluate their corporate balance sheets that are issued by creditors for business loans that could benefit from lesser rates, as well as an improved credit profile.

Let's look at some of the most common types of refinancing.

Rate and Term Refinancing

This is the most common type of refinancing. It usually takes place when the original loan has been paid, and is then replaced by a new agreement that requires lesser interest payments.

Cash Out Refinancing

Cash out refinancing takes place when the asset used as collateral increases in value. During the transaction, the value or the equity of the loan is withdrawn for a higher loan, which often comes with an increased interest rate. Simply put, when the value of an asset increases, you don't have to sell it. Instead, you can take a loan for it. It does increase the loan amount, but it prevents the owner from relinquishing the ownership of their asset.

Cash In Refinancing

Cash-in refinancing allows the borrower to pay a percentage of the loan at a smaller loan to value ratio or smaller loan payments.

Consolidation Refinancing

A consolidation loan is also an effective way to refinance a loan. Such refinancing is possible when the investor lands a loan that has a lower interest rate than the interest rate that exists across various credit products. In this case, the borrower needs to request a loan with a lower interest rate and then pay off the existing debt with the new loan. Hence, they can leave their outstanding principal with a lower interest rate payment.

Now, let's look at some of the benefits of refinancing.

- It provides you with a lower interest rate, and a lower monthly mortgage payment.
- It also allows you to transform an adjustable interest rate into a fixed interest rate, thus ensuring savings and gaining predictability.
- For your pressing financial needs, you can get an influx of cash.
- It enables you to set a shorter loan term, thus paying less money in interest.

Here are some of the downsides of loan refinancing.

- In the event that the loan term goes back to what it was originally, the interest rate will hike to the point where it will outweigh whatever you have saved till that point.

- If you have a fixed rate mortgage, you won't benefit even if the interest rate drops, until and unless you opt for a refinance.
- The equity you hold in your property might also be lost.
- With a shorter loan, your monthly payments will increase and you will end up paying extra money for refinancing.

It is important to note that discrimination in the case of mortgage lending is illegal. There can be times when you feel discriminated against on the basis of color, caste, creed, religion, your political affiliations or your economic background; you have the option to report this discrimination to the Consumer Financial Protection Bureau. You can also go to the US Department of Housing and Urban Development.

Corporate Refinancing

If you don't know already, corporate refinancing is the process in which a business sorts out its financial obligation by replacing or restructuring their current debts. This measure is often used by companies to improve their financial condition. It usually happens when a company is distressed because of debt restructuring. In this process, older corporate bonds are called in, and new ones are issued at a decreased interest rate.

Chapter 7: Best Investments in 2022

The pandemic has taught us numerous lessons. One of those is the importance of being financially fit. In the last two years, we have witnessed businesses shutting down and people facing the height of financial difficulties. But it's not just the pandemic. Having enough money to fall back on is key to having a comfortable financial future.

You shouldn't have to worry about getting up every day and going to work just to put food on your table. If you can carve out a steady source of income other than your job or your business, you won't have to worry about making ends meet, even if things go a little sideways.

Reasons to Invest

Before we get to the crux of this chapter, let's first answer the simple question - why should you invest in the first place? Well, there are several reasons for investing the money you have. Maybe your salary doesn't suffice, and you need an extra income source. You might have to save for your retirement or get yourself out of a financial jam. You might have also just sold a piece of property, and you want your money to work for you.

The great thing about investments is that they appreciate with time, thus giving you the purchasing power you need. Before you can head out and make investments, it is important to balance out the potential gains with some involved risks.

Moreover, while on the road to building wealth, you need to ensure a manageable debt level. You also need a decent emergency fund to utilize without having to access your money if things get difficult.

Let's take a look at some of the best investments in 2022.

Stock Funds

Chances are, you aren't too interested in analyzing individual stocks. If such is the case, you should check out stock funds, whether it is a mutual fund or an ETF. Also, if you buy a more diversified fund such as a Nasdaq 100 index fund or an S&P index 500 fund, you will end up with some very high growth stocks. However, you will have a rather diversified group of companies, as opposed to what will happen if you own only some individual stocks.

Stock funds are great for people who want to use stocks aggressively, but don't have the time to do it as a full-time thing. Moreover, with stock funds, you will end up with the weighted average return of all the companies within the fund. Therefore, a stock fund is less volatile than having only a select few stocks.

However, it is worth noting that if you find it is only confined to a specific industry, it won't be as diversified as funds based on a broader index like the S&P 500. Let's suppose you have stocks in the automobile industry. These stocks are related to prices within the oil industry. Consequently, an increase in oil prices will negatively impact these stocks.

If you weigh the risks and rewards involved with this strategy, you will realize that the chances are 50/50. Sure enough, investing in stock funds is less risky, and little work is involved. However, in extreme situations, you can experience a gain or a loss of 30%. Unlike individual stocks, a stock fund is easier to follow. Moreover, because multiple companies are involved, it is a no-brainer that they won't taste success within the same year. As a result, your returns will remain much more stable.

Growth Stocks

As the name implies, growth stocks offer better returns and better growth. In most cases, growth stocks are tech companies, but they don't always have to be. In most cases, their profits are reinvested into the business. They don't necessarily pay out a dividend until they incur some form of loss or if their growth slows down.

However, these stocks can be somewhat risky. Let's suppose you pay top dollar to acquire the stocks, depending upon the business's reputation and its earnings. All of a sudden, the market goes into bearish mode or a recession arrives. The value of these stocks will take a major hit. On the bright side, growth stocks have proven to be some of the best performers in the long run.

If you plan on buying individual growth stocks, you will have to analyze the company and its performance in detail, and it can take a lot of time. But considering their volatility, you need to have a higher risk tolerance, as well as the commitment to hold the stocks for the next 3-5 years.

Speaking of risks and rewards, these stocks are risky since investors are willing to pay more for them. Consequently, in difficult circumstances, their prices can plummet. On the bright side, if you can find the right company like Amazon or Alphabet, the gains can be endless.

Bond Funds

Whether it is a mutual fund or an ETF, a bond fund contains bonds for a number of different issuers. The bonds within the fund are categorized by factors like the issuer, duration, and riskiness. An issuer could be a corporate organization, a municipality, or a governmental establishment.

When a company or a governmental institution offers a bond, it pays specific interest to the owner of the bond towards the end of the year. By the end of the bond's term, the issuer pays the original amount of the bond, which leads to bond redemption.

A bond in itself is a safe investment, and it becomes even more secure in a bond fund. The reason is, a bond fund contains several bonds that come from a variety of issuers that are stashed across various industries. As a result, the holdings are diversified, and it also lessens the negative impact on bond portfolios in case one of the bonds defaults.

It is true that a bond tends to fluctuate, but a bond fund can remain somewhat stable, even if it responds to the fluctuation of the current interest rates. Moreover, unlike stocks, bonds are considered a safer option. The only problem is, not every issuer is the same. In comparison to corporate organizations, bonds from governmental institutions are considered safer. However, the bond fund's return is less than stock funds. On an annual basis, a bond fund offers a lesser return than a stock fund. Usually, it is 4-5% a year, and in the cases of governmental institutions, it is even less.

Dividend Stocks

Dividend stocks can often have higher returns. However, unlike growth stocks, they aren't as quick. As the name implies, a stock dividend is the one that offers a regular cash payout. There are multiple stocks out there that offer a dividend, but they are most common among mature companies with a little need for cash.

Similarly, they are popular among older investors since they offer a regular income. Interestingly, the dividend continues to grow with time. REIT is one of the most popular examples of dividend stocks.

As far as risks are concerned, just because dividend stocks are less volatile doesn't mean they cannot rise and fall drastically. Things can happen even faster when the stock market enters a rather rough patch. However, unlike a growing company, a dividend-paying company is more mature. Therefore, the process is considered safer.

However, if the dividend-paying company doesn't make enough money, it will surely cut the payout. Consequently, its stocks will plummet, thus creating problems for the investors. The biggest attraction associated with dividend stocks is the payout. A company that pays two to three percent a year can also pay eight to nine percent in the long run as well.

Therefore, you will enjoy a pay raise, basically every year. In the case of dividend stocks, the returns can go up, but they cannot be as great as growth stocks. The good news is that if you are looking for a diverse set of stocks, you can find various kinds available.

Value Stocks

For the past couple of years, the market has been running up. That is part of the reason why stock valuations have been stretched. As a result, people are turning to value stocks. These stocks offer returns while allowing the investors to be as defensive as possible.

When it comes to certain valuation metrics, value stocks prove to be cheaper. One such metric is the price earnings ratio. This metric shows how much investors are paying for each dollar per earning. Unlike growth stocks, value stocks tend to grow slower. However, value stocks can do well this year since they tend to grow, especially when interest rates are on the rise. Such an increase has already been predicted by the income reserve.

The good thing about value stocks is minimized risks. It means that if the market falls, these stocks won't fall too much. Furthermore, if the market conditions are favorable, they can rise well. These stocks work as a double-edged sword. First of all, the chances of loss are negligible, and secondly, they allow you to bag a decent return. What's even more interesting is that some value stocks also pay a dividend, which helps you get some extra returns on your investment.

Target Date Funds

If you don't want to manage your portfolio yourself, it is better for you to opt for target-date funds. With time, these funds become more conservative, thus making your portfolio safer as you age. It helps you even more when you reach retirement and are in need of money. As your target date draws closer, your investments can be shifted from aggressive stocks to conservative bonds.

In a lot of 401(K) plans, target funds are a good choice. However, it is up to you whether or not you want to buy them outside of your plans. The fun part is, all you have to do is to pick a retirement plan, while the fund handles everything else.

Because these funds are a combination of bond funds and stock funds, they have the same risks involved. If the target date is years or decades away, you will find a variety of stocks, which will be volatile in the beginning. However, as the target date approaches, there will be less fluctuation, but you will also earn less.

As discussed above, while moving towards the target date, the fund moves closer to bonds. It means that the bonds will underperform on the stock market. It wouldn't be wrong to say that you will be sacrificing your earning rights for some security. Considering the fact that bonds yield a lesser amount, chances are you will outlive your money. With that in mind, some financial advisors believe it is better to buy a target-date fund that is almost a decade after you plan to retire. As a result, you will get to enjoy some extra growth from the stocks.

Cryptocurrency

Cryptocurrency is a kind of digital currency which is used as a means of exchange. During the last few years, the popularity of cryptocurrencies like Bitcoin has surged. Dollars have jumped into the scene, thus skyrocketing the prices of Bitcoin on numerous occasions. The increase in prices has attracted a sheer number of investors and traders that want to benefit from this digital currency.

For better or for worse, the prices of Cryptocurrency continue to fluctuate. For example, at the beginning of 2020, the Bit coin's price was $10,000. By January 2021, the prices had gone up to $30,000. Then came a time that the value of bitcoin crossed the $60,000 mark before it fell back again. However, 2022 hasn't proven to be a good year for Cryptocurrency. This fluctuation also resulted in a decline in the prices of other digital currencies. With that being said, people who are still holding Cryptocurrency of any kind might be looking at a profit, for it isn't uncommon for Cryptocurrency to fluctuate before rising again.

Cryptocurrency is mostly for people who are adventurous enough to handle its volatility. On the flip side, if you prefer playing it safe without any uncertainty, it is better not to take this route. One of the biggest risks with Cryptocurrency is that it can easily be outlawed by the authorities, which can reduce its prices to zero.

If you still doubt the volatile nature of Cryptocurrency, please note that Cryptocurrency prices can increase and decrease within a short period of time, and these fluctuations take place primarily due to the rate traders are willing to pay.

The reason why traders try to play it safe is that they want to prevent hacking, considering the fact that there have been some high-profile cases of theft in the past. If you are planning on buying Cryptocurrency, it is better to turn to people that have been around for quite some time while others choose to disappear.

Read Estate

It wouldn't be wrong to say that real estate is the archetype of the original long term investment. To get started with real estate, you need a significant amount of money. The returns and the commissions are quite decent in the case of real estate investments. However, it is better to have owned a piece of property for an extended period of time, as opposed to only a few years.

Another great thing about real estate is that it allows you to borrow money from a bank and then pay it back with time. Moreover, the interest rates are low, which is an added benefit.

Furthermore, it allows you to be your own boss while enjoying the tax benefits of being a property owner. In most cases, real estate is considered a passive income option. However, you can turn it into an active one by renting the property.

However, there are some downsides. First of all, by borrowing a considerable amount of money, you put a lot of stress on an investment. Moreover, investing all of the borrowed amount in a singular investment discourages the diversification you are looking for. Also, if you don't have a tenant, you will end up paying maintenance and mortgage costs out of your own pocket.

On the bright side, if you maintain the property well and manage to hold it for a while, you can make good money off of it. If you manage to pay off the mortgage, you can enjoy enhanced stability while making your property more and more attractive to older investors.

Rules for Long-Term Investment

Once you have made up your mind to invest, there are several factors to consider. These factors include your tolerance to risk, the time horizon, your investment knowledge, and your financial situation in terms of how much you can invest. Speaking of risks, you can take fewer risks but the returns won't be as great. However, if you want better returns, you will have to be adventurous enough to take bigger risks.

Risk Tolerance

Yes, you guessed it right. Risk tolerance is the ability to cope with the fluctuations of your investment value. Risk tolerance depends upon your mindset, as well as your financial state to handle risks. Investors that are nearing their retirement tend to be more conservative with their approach. These people can allocate a large part of their portfolio to several low-risk investments. These investments are good for people saving for short-term and intermediate-term financial goals. Even if the market becomes a little volatile, you won't lose your investment.

On the flip side, people that are a decade or two shy of their retirement can have riskier portfolios as long as they keep them diversified. A longer timeline helps you deal well with stock volatility while benefiting from potentially higher returns.

Time Horizons

Time horizon refers to when you need the money. Do you need the money today or 10 years down the line? Do you plan on saving for retirement, or do you want to buy a house? What a time horizon does is that it tells you which investments are appropriate for you and which ones are not.

Let's suppose you have a shorter time horizon. If such is the case, your money should be in your bank account rather than stuck somewhere. Some safe options at your disposal are bonds, savings accounts, and CDs. These options are safer, and they tend to fluctuate a lot less.

However, if you have a bigger time horizon, you can aim for bigger returns, but the investments will be risky and volatile. If you can muster up the courage, you will have to experience the ups and downs of the market, but the profitability will also be higher. If you have more time, you can invest in stocks and hold them for three to five years.

It is worth noting that your investment should be in perfect accordance with your time horizon. You simply cannot invest next month's salary into stocks and expect it to show results the following month.

What Is Your Level of Knowledge?

Your investment knowledge helps you make well-informed and educated decisions in terms of what you are investing in. Investment options such as CDs and savings accounts require minimal knowledge since they are already protected. On the flip side, products such as bonds and stocks need more knowledge. If you want to invest in stocks and bonds, you will have to educate yourself. You will have to conduct in-depth research about the company, the industry, the company's financial conditions, market competitiveness, etc.

However, there are some ways to benefit from the market, even if you don't have sufficient knowledge. Your best bet is an index fund, which happens to include a collection of stocks. Even if one of the stocks underperforms, it will do little to affect the entire index. However, investing in the performance of dozens of stocks is a big gamble, but the gains will surely outweigh the losses if the strategy clicks.

How Much to Invest

The more you invest, the higher will be the risk, but it will also increase your profit margin in the long run. Moreover, bringing in more money will allow you the time you need to understand a specific stock and an industry because the potential rewards are much greater compared to bank products like CDs. Otherwise, it won't be worth your time. You can simply stick with bank products or mutual funds/ETFs that don't need a significant time investment. Such an approach is helpful for people that want to increase their account incrementally, just like 401(k) participants.

Factors to Consider Before Making Investments

What is an investment? Simply put, an investment is a process of putting your money into an asset, hoping to earn a profit. As we have already discussed in this chapter, there are numerous types of assets, and the most popular ones are real estate, stock market shares, and fixed-term deposits. There are several reasons why a person chooses to make an investment decision.

Sometimes, they invest to fulfill personal needs, while sometimes, there is a business that needs funding. Whatever the end goal is, there are several factors one must consider before putting money into an investment. To make your investments easier for you, I have listed down some things you must factor in before making an investment decision.

Return on Investment

A person goes into the market and takes all the necessary risks in order to earn a decent ROI. In the absence of an ROI, investments are fruitless. In the other words, an ROI is the benefit gained by an investor after deducting all the costs of their investments. ROI comes in a number of forms. Sometimes it comes in the form of interest, and sometimes it comes in the form of capital appreciation or dividends. Furthermore, the ROI must be expressed in the form of net income after taxes have been deducted. Also, the net after-tax return must exceed inflation. Lastly, there is always a slight amount of risk involved when it comes to ROI. However, investments with a higher risk level provide the best ROI.

Risk

Let's build upon the point we concluded the previous paragraph with. That right, ladies and gentlemen, risk is another important factor to consider before putting your money in any investment. If you don't know already, risk is the possibility of losing all the money you have invested. As we have discussed, the higher the risk, the higher your chances of making good money, and vice versa. A great example of high-risk investments is shares. There is a great amount of risk involved in shares as opposed to investing in fixed deposits, but they also offer higher returns.

Investment Period

As the name implies, an investment period is a specific investment's length or duration. It plays a huge role in your ROI - something we discussed a few paragraphs ago. Your investments can be medium, long, or short. A long-term investment can be held for more than a year, while a shorter investment can be held for less than a year or a year at max.

Furthermore, long-term investments offer a higher return on investment, unlike the shorter-term investments. It is also worth considering that the duration of an investment depends upon the personal needs of the investor. If the investor is in dire need of cash, they will automatically opt for a shorter loan term, but they end up missing out on a better ROI.

Liquidity

You cannot factor out the liquidity of an asset. Cash is by far the most liquid of all assets. The reason is that cash can be accessed at all times and used on any purchase. The liquidity of an asset is the asset's ability to be converted into cash. If there is an emergency, there must be an amount of capital allocated to the particular investment that can be converted into cash at will.

Real estate is a great long-term investment, and it can yield a higher ROI considering the hike in the prices of property. However, it cannot be easily converted into cash because property takes time before it can be sold. One needs to find the right buyer that can pay the right amount for a piece of land.

On the flip side, a savings account is liquid enough to be converted into cash whenever needed. Similarly, some shares in the stock market are considered liquid because they can be easily sold off to traders on the stock market.

Tax Implications

It doesn't matter who you are, what you do, and your source of income. As long as you are a citizen, you will have to pay your taxes. Tax is the compulsory fee a citizen must pay the government. Your level of taxation also plays a crucial part in your investment decisions. Different investments have different implications as far as taxes are concerned. It is important to factor in all the tax implications before opting for an investment plan. Once you have sorted out all of your taxes, it will become easier for you to earn a better ROI. One of the signs of a good investment is that it offers a good after-tax income. If it doesn't provide a good post-tax income, you must think twice before making an investment.

Inflation Rate

As we all know, inflation is the hike in prices of goods and services which results in the devaluation of money. The rate of inflation is a different story. The inflation rate is a percentage calculated per annum to measure the average increase in prices across the economy.

For example, for the past few years, the rate of inflation in South Africa has been hovering around 4%. So, what does a good investment look like in these circumstances? A good investment helps the investor generate an interest rate of 6% and above to beat the inflation rate while producing visible returns.

An increase in the inflation rate minimizes the purchasing power of the people. A decent investment is the one that provides an ROI that is higher than the current inflation rate. Some investments are positively impacted by an increase in the prices of goods and services. A great example in this regard is real estate.

Whenever there is a hike in prices, the prices of property increase with them. If you have a piece of land lying around somewhere, the best time to sell is when the prices have risen, thus earning a good ROI.

Fluctuations and Volatility

While inflation is the increase in prices, volatility is the condition when there is a continuous rise and fall in prices. A market that experiences a lot of rise and fall in prices is considered a highly volatile market. Low volatility in the market is a good thing because it alludes to stability. Before investing, investors need to take into consideration the fluctuations in the local and international economic trends. Volatility can either make you a profit or a loss, so be wise when making a decision.

Planning Factors for Investment

When making an investment decision, the best thing to do is to look for the safest possible investment opportunities. As we know, some investments don't yield a good ROI, but they are safer in nature and therefore protect your investment. On the flip side, some investments provide bigger profits, but they also come with a lot of risk.

First, you must look for all the investment opportunities with a good return history. Next, in order to minimize risk, your investments should be divided among different investment options. You must also factor in the method of calculating interest.

Budget

No matter how ambitious or intelligent an investor is, they will always revisit their budget before even thinking of investing. But why is the budget so important for an investor? First of all, it enables them to plan out unexpected costs. The budget also helps set money aside for investments, emergencies, and savings.

It also allows them to figure out the percentage of their money that will eventually end up in the form of investments. Devising a well-thought budget is difficult and consumes a lot of time too. However, the good thing about budgeting is that it clarifies the reality of an investor's financial situation, thus enabling them to make wiser decisions and eventually earn bigger profits.

Bad Investment Red Flags

We are impressionable creatures with an innate tendency to be gulled by things that are marketed in the fanciest fashion. While purchasing a product in the supermarket just because it had a catchy advertisement on Facebook might not be so economically damaging, the same cannot be said about investments. In the world of investments, there is no such thing as certainty.

Just because a thing has worked for someone doesn't mean it will work for you as well. So clearly, it is a hit or a miss. Even the safest of investments can turn sour due to market conditions and forces that exist outside your control.

Luckily, some investments carry obvious red flags, so it becomes a little easier for investors not to fall prey to such scams. These investments allow you to be careful before investing, thus enabling you to avoid any potential losses.

To make your investments easier, I have put together for you a list of warning signs/ red flags that will allow you to make safer investments and not fall into a financial trap.

An Advisor Asks You to Invest

Before you disregard any such investment, it is important to know beforehand that because an investment counselor recommends an investment doesn't mean it is bad for you. However, you need to understand that a broker that works for a commission doesn't necessarily need to work as a fiduciary.

It means that it is not a part of their job description to put their client's interests above their own interests. A broker may push you to invest in a particular thing because that investment might make them a higher commission.

Before you make an investment, take a look at how the broker is paid and whether or not the investment will help you in the long run.

You Need to Borrow to Buy It

Some investors are sophisticated. To leverage the effects of an investment, they choose to borrow money. However, this technique is better left for traders dealing in high-risk stocks. If you aren't one of them, you should look for a safer stock that doesn't require you to borrow money to be able to invest.

Unless you can buy an investment outright, there is no need for you to borrow money. If the investment fails, you will end up in debt, and repayment can be a real hassle. Moreover, you also cannot factor out the interest you will pay on your margin loan. Furthermore, the longer the term of your loan will be, the higher the interest you'll end up paying.

Everyone Else Is Buying the Same Thing

As we have discussed, we are impressionable by nature, and we try our best to do what everyone else is doing, just to be able to fit in with the crowd. The same policy doesn't apply in the case of investments. Jumping into an investment just because others are doing it is a big no-no. The same thing happened in the 1600s when everyone tried to buy their way into the tulip craze.

That fad was doomed for failure, to begin with, and it is no wonder that it came to a collapse. It is useful to remember that almost all hot stocks crash once the excitement comes to an end. Instead of buying something that everyone else is buying, it is better to be intelligent about it, and conduct in-depth research, so you can protect your investment.

You Have to Buy It Right Away

There will be people who will try to convince you to buy something before it goes away. This is one of the major red flags that people tend to avoid. This advice may sound old-fashioned at first, but investments that are based on fundamentals are good investments. Even if such investments take weeks, months, or even years to provide you with an ROI, they will be good for you because all the processes will be transparent.

If someone forces you to hand over your money to them as quickly as possible, let it be known that it is nothing but a scam or a hot investment that will burst like a bubble at any time. No matter how long it takes you to reap the fruit, it is always a good idea to stick to fundamental investments where nothing is hidden.

It's Low in Price

Just because an investment is cheaper than the rest and doesn't need enough money from you, it is still risky. Just because something has a lower price doesn't mean that the price won't sink lower.

If you don't know already, most industry professionals refer to the practice of buying cheaper stocks as the act of catching a falling knife. Stocks that experience a sudden price drop often remain at the lower level for a long time, which is frustrating and risky for any investor. The time you waste waiting for the prices to stabilize before you can sell can be used to invest in other options.

All the Rich People Are Buying It

One thing that we fail to understand is that everyone has a different agenda behind buying a stock. Once again, I would urge all of my readers not to buy something unless it is genuinely good for their needs.

We also tend to fall into investment options chosen by some of the richest people on the planet, like Warren Buffet. Just because Warren Buffet is buying something doesn't mean you have to buy it too, or it will work for you the same way it works for him. You don't have the slightest idea what his intentions behind the investment are.

Moreover, even if he fails at an investment, it won't have any effect on his financial situation. But if you fail, things will be pretty different. Therefore, make it a habit of considering investment options that are safe and beneficial for your financial situation.

Stocks Outperform the Company

There are times when a stock skyrockets while its performance remains less than minimal. Such stocks are bad news as they can fall when you expect them the least. Usually, what happens is that the financial performance of the business drives the stocks.

If the business's performance isn't up to par, there is something else that has resulted in a rise, and it won't be long before the prices of those stocks come down once again. Before opting for a specific stock, make sure to do some research and determine its price-to-earnings ratio.

Then look for undervalued or fairly priced investments instead of the ones with a high price-to-earnings ratio.

You Can't Let Go

This is also a major red flag that most people don't pay attention to. Some investments out there force you to hold onto them for a long time before you can let them go. If such requirements are attached to an investment, you should steer clear of them. A perfect example of such investments is variable annuities. These investments have a surrender period; if you sell before that period ends, you will have to deal with charges of almost 5-9%.

It is worth noting that variable annuities aren't completely bad for you, as they have some profitable elements too. However, you must look for alternatives that have no such strings attached.

You Got a Tip

Some of the stocks out there are praised tirelessly by the people trying to promote them. If you find yourself battling with such a situation, it is better to get out of it before it is too late. Such scams often surface after a natural calamity like an earthquake or a flood.

People tend to sell investments by saying that some stocks will skyrocket, while the opposite is possible. Don't invest in such stocks out of desperation. Only opt for the ones recommended by analysts.

It's Too Good to Be True

A sales rep's job is to tell people what they like to hear. Sadly, not all of those things are true, especially in the case of investment. It doesn't mean that all of the investments that sound too good are bad for you. However, some investments have catchy taglines on social media and elsewhere. Most of these investments are better left untouched, as they are scams designed to rob you.

Performance of a Stocks Trails Peers

Stocks, in general, are very diverse. Not only are they traded within their respective industries, but also among different industries. If there is a stock that underperforms its peers, that stock is better left unused, as it can be dangerous for your investment.

These stocks are frequently undervalued, and investing in such stocks can send your investment down the abyss. The undervalued stocks also indicate that the business is being beaten at its own game. To protect your investment and bag a decent ROI, it is better to stick to industry leaders rather than ones that aren't performing well.

You Have Different Objectives for Investing

Before making an investment or even planning one, it is better to ask yourself about the objectives you want to accomplish. Is it the growth of your capital that you aim for, or are you looking for an extra/passive income stream?

It may also be a combination of the two. Each investment type tends to offer a different type of reward. Sometimes, an investment may fall outside your personal parameters. If it does, it is a warning sign, and you should stay away from such an investment.

You Don't Have the Right Risk Tolerance

What is risk tolerance? In simple words, risk tolerance is an investor's ability to deal with market volatility. Do you have the ability to deal with stocks that plunge or rise by 5% every day? Or will you just stand there watching the stock going up and down while the mere sight of it will be extremely disturbing for you?

An investment might seem too good on paper, but if you don't have the financial strength to handle the risk, there is no point in wasting your time and money. It is better to stick to investments that are more stable in nature.

It Worked for You in the Past

As we have already discussed, just because a specific investment worked for you in the past doesn't mean it will work for you again. According to the SEC, past success on a specific stock is by no means a guarantee of future success, so take heed.

I am not asking you to avoid such investments as the plague. All I want you to do is to do your homework well before plunging into an investment that helped you in the past. During this time, the market might have changed, as well as your ability to handle the risks and the challenges involved. An investment that worked wonders for you five years ago could be a disaster now.

It Is Sold by Insiders

Another major red flag is when insiders are selling an investment option. However, these investments are risk-free and profitable in some cases.

What happens typically is that corporate executives are looking for ways to raise cash, and therefore, they try to market these investments to the general public.

However, it does get a little risky when the top leadership is selling large chunks of stocks, and no one on the inside is buying. If such is the case, the investment opportunity is nothing but a scam, and it is better to stay away from it as much as possible.

It doesn't mean you should eliminate these stocks from your list of investment opportunities. Just wait a bit, do your homework, and don't purchase these stocks until you are absolutely certain about their authenticity.

It's Hard for You to Understand

There are some investments out there that are hard to understand to begin with. Some are so complex that you can't even comprehend them in the simplest English. If such is the case, the investment is a scam and nothing else.

An investment that is so arcane will definitely cause some major problems for you down the line. There are so many simpler investments out there with proven results that you don't have to get into something that is hard for you to understand in the first place.

It's Unregistered

Some investments out there are unregistered, and they are best left untouched. In reality, these investments are meant for accredited investors. So, who are these accredited investors? These are the people that possess sufficient income or assets that allow them to make mistakes.

If you are an investor with a limited amount of money to invest, it is pointless for you to get stuck with an investment that isn't even registered. The worst thing about these investments is that just because they are unregistered, they aren't by the same laws of security as other investments.

On the flip side, bonds and stocks that are traded publicly are registered and are governed by some standardized laws that play a big part in the protection of one's investment.

So, unless you are a high-profile investor that can handle such mistakes, it is better to stick with investments that are transparent in nature and offer you better opportunities, and, most importantly, protection.

Making an investment seems fun and games until you face real-world challenges. If you can manage to hold your cool and put in the time and effort to understand the market's inner workings, you can make some good profits.

When making an investment, there are a few things you need to take care of. First of all, always avoid the investments that are sold to you by desperate promoters, as well as the ones that sound too good to be true.

Also, your investment options should be transparent, and they should be governed by laws that protect the investments people put in. Moreover, never buy into an investment only because it has worked for someone, as well as the ones that have worked for you in the past. First, each investor is different, and their motives behind investing differ.

Furthermore, market conditions continue to change with time, and just because an investment worked for you in the past will work for you still. It is better to keep your eyes and ears open to succeed with investments.

Chapter 8: Digital Currencies and NFTs

Contrary to popular belief, digital currency isn't just a means of exchange but a method of generating passive income. But, what is digital currency? Simply put, digital currency is the currency that isn't based on fiat currency. It is a non-tangible currency that serves the same purpose as other currencies, and that is to serve as payment in transactions.

When we talk about digital currencies, the first thing that comes to our minds is cryptocurrency. Cryptocurrency is a payment system that doesn't need banks to carry out and verify transactions. It is a peer-to-peer system that allows anyone to send and receive payments. Unlike physical currencies that sit in your wallet, cryptocurrency payments are digital entries describing specific transactions in an online database. The transactions are recorded in a public ledger, while crypto is stored within digital wallets.

So, where does the name "crypto" come from? This digital currency is called crypto because it needs encryption for the verification of transactions. As a result, some high-level coding is used for the safe transmission of data between public ledgers and wallets. The primary reason behind these encryptions is to provide security.

Bitcoin is the oldest and the most popular cryptocurrency. It was founded in 2009. Trading for better profits is the primary reason why people deal in cryptocurrency. Some other popular cryptocurrencies are as follows.

Litecoin

This currency is similar to Bitcoin in a number of different ways. However, it has grown quickly, as far as innovations are concerned. It offers a faster payment method and also allows a bigger number of transactions.

Ethereum

Being introduced in 2015, Ethereum is relatively a new player in the crypto landscape. Ethereum is basically a blockchain platform and has its own cryptocurrency.

Ripple

Ripple was founded in 2012, and it is a distributed ledger system. Ripple is used to monitor and track different kinds of transactions, and not just crypto transactions. The parent company has worked closely with banks and other financial institutions, thus leading to its popularity.

Ways to Buy Cryptocurrency

Here are some ways to buy cryptocurrencies safely.

Choosing a Platform

There are two platforms to buy cryptocurrency. You can go to a traditional broker or a cryptocurrency exchange.

Traditional Brokers

A traditional broker offers different ways to buy and sell cryptocurrencies and other financial assets like bonds, stocks, and ETFs. With traditional brokers, you can get lower trading costs, but they don't offer lesser crypto features.

Crypto Exchanges

Unlike a traditional broker, a crypto exchange offers cryptocurrencies, interest-bearing account options, and wallet storage. Many of them charge an asset-based fee.

Account Funding

With a platform chosen, you need to make sure you have chosen the right account funding options because then you will be able to trade. There are some platforms that allow their customers to buy crypto with cash or with their credit or debit cards. However, this may vary from one platform to the next.

However, it is worth noting that in some cases, crypto purchases made with credit or debit cards aren't considered safe. However, some exchanges prohibit such dealings in the first place, while some credit card companies also don't approve of it altogether. This is primarily due to the volatile nature of cryptocurrency.

Some platforms also accept ACH and wire transfers. The payment methods and the time taken for each deposit and withdrawal tend to differ from one platform to the other. However, the time it takes for deposits says everything about payment methods.

It is also important to consider the fees. Fees usually include potential deposit, withdrawal transaction fees, as well as trading fees. However, these fees can vary depending upon the platform, as well as the payment method.

Placing Orders

You can easily place an order through your broker's mobile or web platform. To purchase currencies, all you have to do is select "buy" on their platforms. Then, you also have to choose the specific order type. Next up, you tell the system how much crypto you wish to purchase and which one. Luckily, the same process applies to the process of selling cryptocurrencies without any added complexities.

While it is easy to choose a platform, some of the most popular ones are PayPal and CashApp. Moreover, here are some investment vehicles you can consider. Nowadays, Bitcoin Trusts are very popular. Using a regular brokerage account, you can easily purchase the shares of a Bitcoin trust. Such practices open new investments in the crypto markets. These new investors are usually conventional traders trying to get into the crypto market through the stock market.

Next up, there are some crypto mutual funds you can try out. You can even directly invest in crypto directly from the blockchain companies. The fun thing about these companies is that they are experts in the technology behind cryptocurrency and crypto transactions. As a result, you can easily purchase the ETF or the stocks of the company that use blockchain technology.

Making Passive Income with Cryptocurrency

Before moving to the more complex details of crypto, let's talk about ways to earn passive income off of it. Just like any other investment, buying and selling crypto allows you the chance to generate some passive income, which can accumulate with time, thus making you wealthy. As we have already discussed on so many occasions, when you earn passive income on an asset, you tend to profit from something without being directly associated with it. Over here, the same basic principles of reinvesting dividends or compounding interest come into play.

When it comes to making passive income with crypto, you have to choose a method, as well as the amount you want to invest. As discussed a few paragraphs ago, considering the volatile nature of cryptocurrency, there is no exact limit to what is the maximum and the minimum amount of money you are willing to put in. Having said that, people with a bigger investment in crypto will have a higher likelihood of making more money, thus moving a step closer to being wealthy. However, it is always very helpful to weigh the risks when investing. It allows us to endure the risks in case something goes wrong.

Here are some ways to make passive income using cryptocurrency.

Proof of Stake

If you have traded in crypto before, you must have heard the term "proof of stake." Proof of stake is a consensus term used in place of proof of work. Through the Pow network, we figure out which transactions are valid through a process. The process we are talking about deals with nodes that stack up enough tokens. The process of staking also eliminates the process of crypto mining. In POW, it is the miners that tend to receive new block rewards. On the flip side, in the Pops, it is the validators who receive these rewards.

A validator doesn't need some expensive computer hardware. Instead, what they do need is some sufficient tokens to be able to add a block to the blockchain. Before they can allow staking, most networks need an initial investment. If you are looking for crypto options to stake on bigger exchanges, look at Tezos, Cosmos, and Cardano.

Lending

There are many ways for investors to lend out crypto. The idea over here is to give or loan crypto for some time while continuing to receive a fee in exchange. There are three things that determine the amount of time that is earned. Those three things are as follows.

- The loan's duration.
- The interest rate.
- The entire value of crypto being lent.

The higher the rates and the longer the loans, the higher your likelihood of making more money with this investment. There are cases where people that earn from crypto are also the ones making a change in the rules and terms of the loan. If this doesn't happen, there is a third party that negotiates these terms for them.

Let's look at the four different types of lending.

Margin Lending

As the name implies, the act of margin lending happens when we lend to a trader that wants to trade using leverage from the funds they have borrowed. As a result, such loans help traders with the amplification of their position with those assets while they repay their loans with interest. In such cases, most of your details are handled by the crypto exchanges on your behalf. Users need to ensure the availability of their digital assets.

Centralized Lending

This type of lending relies on the lending infrastructure, as well as the terms set by the third party. In these cases, the interest rates are decided and locked ahead of time. Before earning a specific amount of interest, lenders should be able to deposit their crypto amount into the lending platform.

Decentralized Lending

This kind of lending is also known as DeFi lending. In such cases, lending services are accessed directly through the blockchain. Unlike centralized lending, which involves a third party, in the case of decentralized lending, there are no intermediaries, and both the parties interact directly with one another. All of these dealings happen directly over the blockchain. Both the lenders and the borrowers tend to interact through smart contracts, which exist for the purpose of automating interest rates.

Peer to Peer Lending

There are some platforms out there that allow peer-to-peer lending. As the name implies, this model allows people to borrow their decided amounts directly from one another. To begin with, a lender deposits his crypto amount into the custodial wallet of the lending platform. Once they have deposited this amount, they can set the terms of the loan, and the interest rate while determining how much they are actually willing to lend. This model gives users great control over the process of lending cryptocurrency.

Interest-Bearing Digital Assets Account

This account, in some ways, is similar to a savings account. There are multiple service providers out there that allow their users to deposit their crypto amount while earning a yield on it. This method is something new and fresh for most investors since the conventional savings account yields have literally stooped lower than expected during the last couple of years.

To follow this path, all you have to do is open an account and deposit your crypto into it. However, there is a lockup period when the users aren't allowed to access their funds. It can be a little uncertain for the time being, but it starts to pay when the time is right. In exchange for the amount they have deposited into their accounts, they earn interest.

Cloud Mining

All of us have heard of cloud mining, but what is it? When you mine proof of work cryptocurrencies, you need some deep-level technical knowledge. Luckily, cloud mining offers an easy alternative to all of these complexities. With cloud mining, you don't have to put time and money into a mining rig. All one needs to do is rent some hashing power. The hashing power mostly comes from an established operation. For a fixed sum of money, people can easily buy cloud mining contracts. Such a contract allows a person to earn a hash rate over a brief period of time. The owner of the contract tends to receive new coins, depending upon their contract size. However, you must heed the warning. There are so many cloud mining scams out there that exist for the sole purpose of robbing people. Therefore, before you walk down this path, it is important to conduct some in-depth research.

Sun Exchange

With time, solar-powered machines have become increasingly popular. But what is Sun Exchange, and what is all this fuss about? As the name implies, sun exchange is a South African company that crowdsources funding specifically for solar projects. The people involved in this model can buy solar cells. After the solar cells start working and generating results, they can start collecting their payouts. It is up to the users whether they want to use Crypto or they want to do it using fiat currency.

On the same measure, their payouts will also be paid either in fiat currency or in crypto. What differentiates between this method of passive income and others is that it is extremely tangible in itself. Despite being a safe and secure passive income method, the payouts are small and periodic. As a result, they take much longer to accumulate, unlike in other investment methods.

Yield Farming

Between the years 2020 and 2021, decentralized exchanges have become popular. As a result, the idea of yield farming has come in. Decentralized exchanges rely primarily on liquidity, as well as smart contracts provided by the investor. To make money from this technique or to yield farm, the investors have to deposit their coins into what's called the liquidity pool.

The people who provide liquidity tend to receive a small portion of the fees. These fees are generated when traders access the pool. Yield farming is one of the most profitable passive income methods on this list. However, to be able to benefit from it, one needs to conduct some detailed research.

Affiliate Programs

Affiliate programs tend to exist for a variety of different models. One of those models includes products and services related to crypto. Here is what you need to do.

- Sign up, fill out an initial form, or provide the system with an affiliate link for experience and professional accolades.

- Next up, you have to introduce a product or a service to your friends, family, and other people within your social circle.
- Every time someone takes action or signs up for whatever you offer, you will be paid a small portion.

A great example is that of Coinbase. When the time for publishing, Coinbase tends to offer a small incentive to the employees who agreed to bring on a new person to check out a new business, while signing up to their affiliate link. While affiliate programs aren't the only ways to make passive income, it is indeed one of the easiest.

Sun Exchange

With time, solar-powered machines have become increasingly popular. But, what is Sun Exchange, and what is all this fuss about. As the name implies, sun exchange is a South African company that crowdsources funding specifically for solar projects. The people involved in this model can buy solar cells. After the solar cells start working and generating results, they can start collecting their payouts. It is up to the users whether they want to use Crypto or they want to do it using fiat currency.

On the same measure, their payouts will also be paid either in fiat currency or in crypto. What differentiates between this method of passive income and others is that it is extremely tangible in itself. Despite being a safe and secure passive income method, the payouts are small and periodic. As a result, they take much longer to accumulate, unlike in other investment methods.

Ways to Store Cryptocurrency

Just like any other asset, once you have bought some cryptocurrency, you need to make sure it is safe from all hacks and thefts. Usually, the best place to store cryptocurrency is a crypto wallet. Crypto wallets exist both online and offline. They contain keys to your cryptocurrency that only you can use. Some exchanges out there offer wallet services. As a result, it becomes easier for you to store directly through the platform you are using. Let's look at some of the crypto wallet storage types.

Hot Wallet Storage

A hot wallet storage system is one that uses online software to keep keys that protect your cryptocurrency.

Cold Wallet Storage

As the name implies, cold wallet storage depends on hardware, as opposed to an online one. These systems depend upon offline tools used to ensure the security of your keys.

Pros and Cons of Making Passive Income with Crypto

Here are some of the benefits of using crypto as passive income.

- The best thing about using crypto as a means of passive income is the simplicity of the options available to you. The great thing is that most digital asset accounts are simple and straightforward to understand. In most cases, users tend to deposit stable coins and start earning an interest which can pile up into a larger amount with the passage of time.
- As far as centralized lending is concerned, it has more to do than simply putting your crypto into a digital custodial wallet. One of the benefits of centralized lending is that it allows the borrower to lend out the same amount. Such a technique can be very financially beneficial to the original lender.

Now, let's talk about some of the downsides of using crypto as passive income.

- When dealing with crypto with the aim of making money, most of the options come with various risks. In some cases, things can go from bad to worse to a point where you can lose 100% of your principal amount. It usually happens due to hacks, lending platforms going bankrupt and small contractual bugs.

- Then, there are some options that are very difficult to navigate. If you take the DeFi route, you will have to establish and use an Ethereum wallet. A great example is that of MetaMask. With that out of the way, you have to get the hang of the DeFi protocols. If you don't hold the Eth yet, things can get extremely challenging for you. It can also be challenging for those who haven't used digital wallets in their life.

There are many ways a crypto trader can use digital currency to generate passive income for himself. These activities can range from straightforward deposit accounts as well as more complex activities such as running nodes.

The best and the worst thing about cryptocurrency is its volatility. Either it can go extremely high, or it can go down the drain, thus wasting people's investments. When investing in crypto, it is extremely important to conduct in-depth research.

What Are NFTs

These days, NFTs are the talk of the town. But what are these NFTs anyway? Well, NFT is an acronym that stands for non-fungible tokens. Simply put, NFTs are digital assets representing real-world things like music, art, videos, and games. These tokens are sold online, and they tend to use the same encoding system that is used in the case of many cryptocurrencies.

It may sound a little strange, but NFTs have been around since 2014. However, they are becoming increasingly popular now. For most people, it is a shock, but in 2021, the value of the entire NFT market hiked to a record $41 billion. This amount is just a few thousand dollars shy of competing with the value of the global fine arts market.

Each NFT is unique and also has unique identifying codes. They also have a limited run, which can pave the way for digital scarcity. The scarcity factor is what differentiates between NFTs and other digital creations because the latter is abundant in supply. As a result, a decline in supply will automatically increase the value of these NFTs.

One question that is frequently thrown in is the differences between NFTs and cryptocurrencies. The biggest similarity between cryptocurrencies like Bitcoin and Ethereum is that they both use the same programming, but that is where the similarities come to an end.

Unlike NFTs, cryptocurrencies are both fungible, but what does that mean? It means that both crypto and real currency can be traded for one another. Moreover, they are also similar in value. For example, one dollar is equal to another dollar, or a Bitcoin is equal to another Bitcoin. However, the same cannot be said of

NFTs. The fungible nature of cryptocurrency is what makes it a trustworthy means of exchange over the blockchain.

An NFT is different. Every NFT has a unique digital signature, making it impossible to be traded in exchange for another NFT. For example, an NBA top shot clip isn't equal to an EVERYDAYS, just because they are NFTs. Moreover, when you delve deeper, you will realize that even two NBA top shot clips aren't equal to one another.

How Do NFTs Function

An NFT exists on the blockchain. The blockchain is like a digital ledger used for the purpose of recording transactions. If you are familiar with crypto, you might know about the blockchain. In most cases, NFTs are held on the Ethereum blockchain. However, they can be held on other blockchains as well.

As we have already discussed, an NFT is minted in the form of a digital object which represents both intangible and tangible items. Some of the most common examples are as follows.

Arts

Art is the most popular form of NFTs out there. This is part of the reason why art sells so well. The advent of NFTs was a great opportunity for artists all over the globe to sell their work online. In fact, the most expensive NFTs out there are pieces of art. Studies have shown that the most expensive NFT that has been sold till date is known as EVERYDAYS: THE FIRST 5000 DAYS.

This piece of art was sold for a staggering $69 million. Pieces of video art are also becoming increasingly popular on the NFT spectrum. GIFs and short videos are also selling for millions of dollars. One of the most expensive short videos was sold as an NFT for $6.6 million. The video depicted a naked Donald Trump. Surprisingly, the small video wasn't any longer than a few seconds.

Music

The next most popular form of NFTs comes in the form of music. Music has been a fungible item for decades. It has been sold and distributed in the form of cassettes, CDs, and vinyl records ever since recording technology came in. However, since the advent of NFTs, musicians and recording artists have started making millions of dollars in a matter of hours.

When it comes to remuneration, an artist only manages to keep only a small percentage of their proceeds. The rest goes to all of the peripherals and the overheads involved. In the case of NFTs, an artist gets to keep 100% of the total amount without having to pay a dime to anyone. Therefore, a large population of artists is adopting this profitable approach.

Collectibles and Trading Cards

One can also look at NFTs as trading cards. We all know about baseball trading cards that are sold for thousands of dollars. There isn't much difference between NFTs and those trading cards. The difference is, people can easily purchase and trade virtual trading cards as if they are the real thing.

Moreover, just like tangible trading cards, some of them can be sold for millions of dollars. It's not just the trading cards that can be traded in the form of NFTs. Companies are also trading collectible items. If you deem something collectible, it can actually be placed in the NFT market.

Video Game Items

Video game items also hold great value within the NFT market. Don't get me wrong. Organizations aren't selling entire video games. However, they are selling skins, in-game content, and game characters. These days, several copies of DLC assets are also being sold to players. However, each NFT will be unique and exclusive to a single buyer. For developers, it is possible to sell regular DLC. However, for the NFT market, they can only sell an edited version.

Memorable Sports Moments

The great thing about NFTs is that they are used for selling thongs that don't have a physical alternative. A great example of such priceless things is memorable sports moments. These NFTs showcase snippets from some of the greatest moments in international sports history. It could be a game-winning touchdown or a historic slam dunk. A 10-second snippet can easily be sold for more than $200,000.

Memes

The internet is more interesting than you think it is. The NFT market also allows you to trade memes. It gets even more interesting because the person selling the meme can also appear in one. Some of the most popular memes on the NFT market are Disaster Girl, Bad Luck Brian, and Nyan Cat. These memes can range between $30,000 and $770,000. Till date, the most expensive meme on the NFT market has been the Doge meme which sold for a record $4 million.

Virtual Fashion

All the things sold on the NFT market are virtual in nature, and fashion shouldn't be an exception. In the case of NFTs, you won't be wearing a nice t-shirt you just splurged on. However, you will be dressing up your avatar, and that is the fun thing about it. Moreover, if you think someone won't spend millions of dollars on virtual fashion, you are highly mistaken. If people can spend $4 million on a meme, there will be fashion enthusiasts out there ready to pay top dollar for a piece of virtual fashion. However, such items are available in a limited amount on the NFT market.

Domain Names

Domain names have also gotten into the fold of NFTs. You can create a unique domain name and sell it on the NFT market, and by doing so, you can bag an enormous amount of profitability. Usually, when you make and register a domain name, you end up paying a third-party company to manage that domain name. On the flip side, when you buy a domain name on the NFT market, you will end up keeping all the rights, thus subtracting all the middlemen you would pay otherwise.

Miscellaneous Items

There was a time these other miscellaneous items were easy to define. However, during the past year, the NFT market has literally become a digital wild west, where everything is up on offer. These items include Facebook posts, Facebook stories, Instagram stories, and the list goes on. For now, these things are only seen as collectibles. Some real NFT use cases are likely to emerge in the future.

The NFT Advantage

What blockchain really does is that it allows artists and other creative enthusiasts a landscape where they can sell their work without having to sell their rights to anyone. While their work gets monetized, they aren't dependent on any galleries and auctions to sell their work for them and keep a percentage of their proceeds. As a result, the artists have the opportunity to sell their work directly to consumers while enjoying whatever profits they can make upon sale.

Moreover, NFTs also offer sufficient royalties to the artist every time their pieces are sold. NFTs can also be a great source of passive income, and that is part of the chapter too. But we will get to that later. Furthermore, as we have discussed earlier, art isn't the only form of NFTs out there. There are brands out there that sell themed NFTs, which allow them to raise funds for charitable purposes.

How to Purchase NFTs

If you are serious about starting your own NFT project, there are a few things you need to know. First of all, you will need an NFT wallet that serves as a storage space for your non-fungible tokens and your cryptocurrencies. Moreover, you will need to buy some cryptocurrency, such as Ether. Your choice of crypto depends upon the specific currency that your NFT provider supports. Crypto can either be bought using a credit card or platforms such as PayPal, eToro, Kraken, and Coinbase. From these exchanges, you can easily move crypto to the wallet of your choice.

Let's look at some of the most popular marketplaces for NFTs.

OpenSea.io

When it comes to NFT sales, OpenSea.io is actually a market leader. This platform is home to all kinds of digital assets. All you have to do is sign up and check out the items on offer. Moreover, if you are an artist, OpenSea offers a simple and self-explanatory process for you to sell your NFTs. Interestingly, OpenSea accepts more than 150 tokens as payment options, and therefore, its name is appropriate. If you are new to NFTs, OpenSea is the place for you.

Rarible

Just like OpenSea, Rarible is another comprehensive marketplace for NFTs, and it accepts a variety of tokens. This platform is open for buying, selling, and creating all kinds of art, music, and collectibles. However, unlike OpenSea, to buy and sell on Rarible, you have to use their own tokens. Moreover, THIS platform is built on the Ethereum blockchain. However, you can manage your artwork on OpenSea, using Rarible tokens.

Foundation

What's unique about Foundation is that in order to post your work, you need invites or upvotes from other artists or fellow creators. Moreover, you need to purchase gas for minting your NFTs, i.e., boasting high-quality artwork. For example, Chris Torres, the founder of the Nyan Cat meme, sold his NFT on Foundation. This could equate to paying a higher price, but it's not necessarily a bad thing for artists. It allows them to capitalize on the demand for their NFTs.

The great thing about these platforms is that they are home to some of the best collectors and artists. However, it is better for you to conduct in-depth research before buying. One of the major downsides of these platforms is that some impersonators can easily come in. There have been instances where artists have fallen prey to these impersonators when somebody listed their work and sold it under a false name.

Moreover, the verification process also varies from one platform to the next. In fact, some platforms have more stringent verification processes than others. Rarible and OpenSea do not need owner verification for an NFT listing. Moreover, buyer protection is also sparse. Therefore, it is important to keep your eyes and ears open to be able to protect your investments.

Using NFTs for Passive Income

Here are five effective ways to make passive income out of NFTs.

Rent OUT Your NFTs

One of the easiest ways to make money from your NFTs is to rent them out, and especially the ones that are high value. For example, there are some games out there that allow users to borrow trading cards, which enhances their likelihood of winning. The deal between the two parties is governed using smart contracts.

As a result, NFT users have the freedom to decide a specific duration for their rental period as well as the leasing rate for their NFTs. One of the most common examples that comes to mind is reNFT. It is a platform that enables lenders to decide daily rates while setting borrowing periods. Speaking of rates, on average, they tend to range somewhere between 0.002 and 2 wrapped Ethereum.

Stake NFTs

The great thing about combining decentralized financing and NFTs is that it allows you to stake NFTs. But what does staking mean anyway? Staking is the process of locking away your digital assets into a DeFi contract, which helps generate a yield. Some platforms are supportive of a wide range of non-fungible tokens. Then there are those that require you to purchase native NFTs to be able to earn staking token rewards.

Some of the most popular platforms that support NFT staking include Splinterlands, Only1, NFTX, and Kira Network. In some cases, governance tokens denominate a small percentage of the rewards awarded to the stakers. The token holders are empowered by these protocols, thus providing them voting rights for the development of their ecosystems in the future. Moreover, it is also possible to reinvest coins one has earned from NFT staking into other protocols which generate yields.

NFT Royalties

The underlying technologies that guide NFTs allow the creators to set royalty rates when their NFTs change hands. As we discussed above, creators can continue to earn passive income each time their NFTs are sold on the secondary market. As a result, they can earn a share of the sales price of their NFTs indefinitely.

Let's suppose you are a creator who has set a 10% royalty fee for their NFT's sales price. No matter how many times your NFT is sold on the secondary market, you will continue to earn`10% of the sales price. It is worth mentioning that these royalty fees are set at the minting stage. Moreover, the process is completely automated. As a result, you don't have to enforce your track payments or royalty terms manually.

Providing Liquidity

Another great thing about the integration between DeFi infrastructures and NFTs is that it allows liquidity, thus receiving NFTs and establishing their place within a liquidity pool. For example, every time a user provides liquidity on the Uniswap V3, the AMM issues an ERC-721 token, aka LP-NFT. It details your share of the total amount locked within the pool. There are other bits of information that are etched into the NFT include token symbols, the deposited token pair, and the pool's address. In order to liquidate your position in the pool, you can also sell the NFTs.

Do You Need to Buy NFTs

Just because you can afford to purchase NFTs does not mean you are bound to do so. In some cases, NFTs can be risky. There is not much history available, and therefore, it can be difficult to predict their future performance. However, if you must invest in

NFTs, it would be better to start slowly. You can invest smaller amounts in the beginning to test the waters before taking the leap of faith to invest a higher amount.

If you have enough money to splurge, and if a specific piece is meaningful to you, you should definitely invest in a token or two. However, it is worth noting that the value of an NFT depends upon the value someone is willing to pay for it. Therefore, the price will be driven by the demand rather than the fundamental, economic, or technical factors which are crucial to stock prices.

It means that an NFT can re-sell for a lesser amount than what you paid for it, and in some cases, it might not be sold if no one wants to buy it. Moreover, NFTs can also present you with capital gains taxes, which is similar to what happens when you sell stocks at a higher price than what you purchased them for.

However, because they fall within the category of collectibles, they might not be subject to the same preferential tax gain that applies to stocks. Instead, they might be taxed at a collectibles tax rate, even though the IRS hasn't yet made it clear why NFTs should be considered for tax purposes.

It is also worth remembering that the crypto used to purchase these NFTs may also be taxed if they increase in value. Before adding NFTs to your portfolio, it is better to consult a tax professional. With that being said, just because NFTs are risky, it doesn't mean you shouldn't try them out. If you are confident enough, you must approach them, but approach them in a way you would approach any other form of investment. Do your research well, and factor in all the risks and opportunities.

Top NFT Myths Debunked

As we have already discussed, NFTs are a new concept in the digital landscape. That is part of the reason why not many people know what they are, how they function, and how profitable they can be. As a result, we see a sheer number of myths surrounding NFTs surfacing every day. It's even sadder to see how a large chunk of the population falls for these myths. It is also due to a lack of awareness about these digital assets. However, I want to bust all of these myths through this book so no one can trick you into believing in them anymore.

NFTs Are Nothing but Digital Art

For the time being, most NFTs that have been sold are mainly artwork. Pieces of artwork sold as NFTs are also a hot topic of discussion. This is also one of the reasons why people only identify art pieces as NFTs above everything else. It all started when Beeple's "Everydays, The First 5000 Days" was sold in an auction at Christie's. This sale really opened the eyes of the people to the concept of non-fungible tokens. This specific art piece was sold for a staggering $69 million.

To be honest, we cannot really blame anyone for spreading the misconception that NFTs are nothing but different kinds of artwork. It was only a natural outcome of what they had seen. However, the truth is that anything that is digital in nature has the potential to fall within the NFT category.

For example, in-game assets such as weapons and skins are also being minted, and they are sold in the form of non-fungible tokens. Moreover, social media posts, tweets, and even stories on Snapchat can also be sold as NFTs. In the case of NFTs, the sky's the limit, as there is no limit to the creativity this newfound landscape offers to those who have the skills and the desire to capitalize on this technology.

However, there is one thing you need to remember. Everything that is represented by NFTs cannot be stored on the blockchain. Only the NFTs that fall within the Ethereum ER 721 token can be stored on the blockchain. An NFT merely represents an asset that exists somewhere far away from the blockchain itself. For example, a time may come when we'll store our passports or ID card details on the blockchain in the form of NFTs. Our passports or ID cards will still stay with us, away from the blockchain, as tangible items.

The NFT won't replace tangible passports or ID cards. Instead, they will only serve as proof of your important documents. It is a fact that at the moment, the majority of the NFTs in existence are all artwork, and this is how it will be for the next few years, but the day is not far when things like intellectual properties, copyrights, and even the everyday home chores and deeds will be stored onto the blockchain in the form of non-fungible tokens.

It Is Just a Fad

Just like any new technology, people believe that NFTs are just a fad that will fizzle out with time. While this might be true in some cases, considering the potential these digital assets have to offer, I personally feel these assets will one day become a crucial component of the digital spectrum. Well, that is something that is attached to any new technology.

Twenty-five years ago, people said the same thing about the internet. Two and a half decades down the line, we cannot even imagine a life without the internet. The same thing happened to digital marketing when it started a little over a decade ago. Both marketing managers on the client-side and the media planners on the agency end were skeptical about incorporating digital marketing into their strategies, but they were all proven wrong. The same basic principle applies to NFTs.

If not thousands, there are hundreds of use cases for NFTs at the moment. And if I can trust my intuition, I can safely say that NFTs are here to stay, and they will continue to grow in popularity and profitability. While most people look at NFTs as a minor digital novelty, they will be proven wrong since it isn't possible for NFTs to just disappear overnight.

As we have discussed earlier in the chapter, in 2021, the value of the NFT market stood at a record $41 billion. Moreover, this market is catching up with the international art market at a rampant pace. We also cannot factor out the interest of some of the corporate sector's biggest names in these newfound assets. The best example from the top of my mind is none other than Nike. Nike has come up with a system known as CryptoKicks that is based on the NFT technology. This new tool helps a person test the authenticity of their trainer.

When people say NFTs are a fad that will die out with time, they aren't 100% wrong. However, this doesn't apply to ALL NFTs. There are some NFTs out there that will lose value with time. However, most of them will sustain themselves and grow.

NFTs Are a Get-Rich-Quick Scam

There are numerous people with conspiracy theories regarding NFTs. These conspiracies exist to establish that NFTs are nothing but a get-rich-quick scheme, or they are some complex cyber scam that allows a person to make millions of dollars without doing anything or putting in any effort.

Once again, these ideas are based on the same notion that the demand for NFTs is nothing but a bubble that will burst at any time. Moreover, people also believe that when it all ends, there will be *some* winners and *many* losers. Long story short, most people live with the notion that the rug will soon be pulled out from under the feet of those people who have invested in NFTs.

These complaints against NFTs are extremely childish, but it was meant to be like this, considering the results that have rolled out during the past couple of years. While some of the artists selling their NFTs are getting rich, most are not. If NFTs were a scam or a rug pull, most people buying and selling NFTs would have been rolling in money right now. But that isn't happening lately. It is a tell-tale sign that non-fungible tokens are 100% authentic, and to make it big trading them, one needs a lot of hard work and experience.

Moreover, NFTs might be sold at a much lower price in the coming years, but thinking of them as part of a big game doesn't make sense. To put it simply, think of NFTs as diamonds or emeralds. If many people wake up tomorrow and decide to deem precious stones worthless, their opinions won't change the facts. The same has been said about gold, but no one can debate the power of gold. The same applies to NFTs. Just like gold, precious stones, and real estate, its value can fluctuate, but not to the point where it is completely eliminated.

Warren Buffet of Wall Street once jokingly said about gold that it sits there, does nothing, and the best you can do is sit there looking at it and admiring its beauty. But the same cannot be said about NFTs. In fact, these non-fungible tokens have countless real-world uses that gold can never fulfill. Yet people chase after gold as if it has descended from the heavens above. Why in their right mind would they not capitalize on the power of NFTs once they learn how productive they can be?

On social media, many people badmouth NFTs as if it is a large scam that is part of a large scheme known as the Pyramid Scheme. To put a cherry on top, some of them even believe that it is some form of a cult practice that pays an individual only when they bring more people on board. Of all the conspiracy theories about NFTs, this is by far the strangest and the funniest.

The truth is, there is no centralized company out there that is governing the sale and purchase of these assets, and there is not one person that is compelling people to sell NFTs at their behest for a small chunk of the revenue. While NFTs are a new technology and have the potential to yield immense profitability, some people out there want to use them for their illegitimate motives. Some wrongdoers can make quick money off of these assets because it is fairly simple to create a new PFP collection promising to be a Bored Ape or Crypto Punk. This is one of the reasons people who invest in NFTs carry out a comprehensive DD, which stops them from being scammed.

They Are Bad for the Environment

The misconception that NFTs are somehow bad for our environment has also led to a lot of heated discussions online (looking at you, Twitter). While climate changes are a threat to all living species, there is certainly no sense in investing in something bad for the environment. With that being said, neither NFTs nor their minting process has anything to do with harming the environment. Moreover, the minting or trading of NFTs doesn't use too much energy - not as much as mining cryptocurrency does.

The Ethereum blockchain uses a lot of energy when trading and minting NFTs. However, not every blockchain is based on Ethereum's proof-of-work consensus mechanism. Others use a proof-of-stake mechanism instead to process transactions. Some of the most common examples in this regard are Tezos and Cardano. These systems use less energy than Ethereum when minting and trading NFTs.

The sad part is, a majority of NFT transactions take place on Ethereum. This is one of the reasons why NFTs have gained the poor reputation of somehow being a threat to the environment. However, it is also a fact that all these things will change at some point in the future, and that too for the better.

Most people dealing in NFTs at the moment are waiting for the time when Ethereum's proof-of-work systems merge with Beacon. After that, Ethereum will consume almost 99.95% less energy than it currently does. The new Ethereum will be referred to as "Ethereum 2.0," but for the time being, it is only known as The Merge. So, once this much-awaited merger takes place between the two, the misconceptions about NFTs being somehow a threat to the environment will die out.

More solace comes from the fact that crypto mining has become much more energy-efficient than it was in the past. However, according to some stats from the Bitcoin Mining Council, more than 70% of the energy needed for crypto mining comes from sustainable resources. It means that a sheer percentage of energy needed for crypto mining comes from renewable resources.

NFTs are Useless and Worthless

Some people out there believe that NFTs are utterly worthless and a waste of time. Typically, if a person believes in the value of an art piece, it will automatically enhance the value of the NFT that alludes to that specific work of art. So, as the old saying goes, beauty lies in the eyes of the beholder. So, when people deem a specific NFT worthless, they mean that the piece of art backing that NFT will eventually lose its value, which is somewhat true. But because one art piece will become invaluable doesn't mean that the entire concept of digital assets is useless.

If you don't know much about how digital assets work, you need to be able to distinguish between a digital token and the piece of art it represents. They are two very different concepts, and they cannot be used interchangeably. It is certainly debatable whether or not an NFT artwork will be able to sustain its value in a digital database. However, the entire market for these tokens is so big that you cannot dis them simply because someone called them worthless.

At the moment, a majority of NFTs are being used for art or music. However, the use cases will increase in the future, and they will penetrate every industry that one can think of. For example, hospitals will use NFTs to secure their patient records or ID verifications. This will make it much easier for medical centers around the world to collaborate on a deeper level without any discrepancy.

Moreover, NFTs will also be used by individuals to store their IDs, academic documents, and professional credentials, thus making it easier for them to transport them across borders. Most celebrities will also capitalize on this technology as tickets to their big events such as concerts, thus eliminating the possibility of ticket scalping. With so much hidden potential, calling NFTs useless is utterly mindless.

NFTs Are Easily Copied

There are people who think NFTs can easily be copied, resulting in art forgery. This seems far from true. As far as digital art is concerned, it has been around for quite some time now, and it has always faced the right-click and save-as problem. In other words, it is fairly easy to download a video, an image, or audio from the internet so that it can be used elsewhere.

While NFTs help solve this problem by proving ownership and protecting digital artwork, some scammers out there can re-upload artwork as NFTs and make money off of them. So, how does one determine whether or not their owned NFT or the one they choose to buy is an original? Well, the easiest solution to this problem is to conduct in-depth research before handing over the money to someone, irrespective of which exchange they are purchasing the NFT from.

The only possibility of getting duped when buying from an authentic exchange is when you don't do the necessary homework. However, in order to understand why it is difficult to steal NFT art, you need to understand how the blockchain works. A blockchain is a ledger not too different from an accounting ledger, and it is used for storing basically any information that needs to be stored.

However, what differentiates a blockchain from other databases is that the data stored on a blockchain is immutable. It means that the data stored on a blockchain cannot be forged. No one has the power to change or rewrite the bits and pieces of information that you store on a blockchain.

As a result, whenever an NFT artwork is stored and minted on the blockchain, one knows when the action took place and by whom. While it is possible to mint an NFT that looks identical to the original one, identifying the original one is child's play for someone who has spent time on the blockchain and knows how these digital assets function.

Prevention of any kind of forgery is the primary advantage NFT technology has over tangible paintings and drawings. Moreover, the sheer abundance of fake art pieces out there is a major issue that museums and art galleries face. It gets even worse because it is almost impossible to distinguish between an original art piece and a fake one. It sounds weird, but according to a study carried out in 2010, more than 20% of the paintings showcased in museums are fake.

So, while it is possible to duplicate an NFT art piece, just like making a fake copy of the Mona Lisa, it is easy to tell whether or not an NFT art piece is original or fake. Like the world of fine arts, even on the digital landscape, you will find actors trying to scam other people through their fake art pieces. However, it is your responsibility to stay alert and not allow them to take advantage of you. The best thing to do is spend some time with people who are well-versed with digital assets and ways to protect those assets. Don't make the mistake of entering the NFT market without complete information. If you do, you might face a loss that is hard to recover.

NFTs Help Criminals Launder Money

Most regrettably, crypto has developed a reputation of being a means of exchange along the Silk Road, where you can buy anything from firearms to drugs and a lot more. It's even sadder that the connotation of unfairness associated with crypto has bled onto NFTs. As a result, people are skeptical about this newfound fortune, and that is part of the reason why this resource is highly unexploited.

Some people even say that tax evaders and cartels are using NFTs as a medium to transfer money throughout the world. But is this really true? Let's talk about this in detail. The impact of money laundering on the world's economy is somewhere between $800 billion and $2 trillion. Most of this money is stored in offshore banks. Don't get me wrong. Offshore banking is a legitimate practice, and businesses and individuals use it all across the globe. However, it is a fact that numerous criminals are using it to preserve the wrong kind of money in a different country, just so it doesn't get noticed by the authorities.

The best thing for criminals is that offshore banks do not disclose their details to anyone unless they are in an emergency. Such policies are very comforting for the bad guys as it gives them protection. However, in recent times, publications like the Panama and Pandora papers have exposed a lot of big business people and politicians that have hidden their money abroad. These papers provide insights into who has their money in offshore accounts and how much. It is hard to say how this information got out, but it has certainly created a huge buzz, and sadly, it has blemished the reputation of NFTs.

So, how much of the laundered money came from crypto or NFTs? Well, according to research, money from crypto and NFTs equates to almost $8.6 billion, which is less than 1% of the total laundered money globally. The truth is, money launderers have been using whatever means they can get their hands on to protect their money long before the birth of crypto. Moreover, with the help they get from traditional banking practices, they don't even struggle now.

For example, not too long ago, HSBC was fined almost $2 billion for the part it played in a money-laundering scandal that involved Colombian and Mexican drug cartels. Moreover, HSBC wasn't even the only offender in this case. Banks such as Standard Chartered and Goldman Sachs have also padded billions of dollars for the money laundering scandals they have been involved in. One can clearly see that the role of crypto in helping criminals launder cash is less than negligible. As a result, the evidence is not sufficient to completely cancel the effectiveness of crypto or NFTs just because a few people used them for their dark motives.

Buying an NFT Makes You the Owner of the Underlying Asset

Once again, this is not at all true. Just because you own an NFT doesn't mean you now own the asset that the specific NFT represents. This misconception arises primarily due to a lack of technical understanding. When a person buys an NFT, he doesn't automatically take possession of the underlying asset. In fact, unless there is an agreement between the buyer and the seller, the ownership of the original item will remain with the individual who made the NFT.

Let's suppose you purchase a Cryptopunk. Just because you are the buyer, you don't have the right to start producing a range of Cryptopunks. You can only do so when given the go-ahead from the original seller. The intellectual rights will always stay with the original owners. Similarly, just because you purchase a music-related NFT doesn't give you the right to sell your own music under the same record label.

However, in some cases, the purchase of an NFT does provide you with certain rights, depending upon the terms of the sale. But that happens rarely, and in the case of an NFT purchase, you won't get any share of the intellectual rights associated with those NFTs. Moreover, when the NFT is sold on the secondary market, the original owner will receive the royalty for it. Whether it is sold once or ten times in a row, the original owner will continue to earn passive income. But before you can make money off your NFT, you will have to conduct in-depth research so you don't get scammed.

Chapter 9: Having Faith in a Financial Crisis

When times get tough, it is easy for even the staunchest of believers to give in to the frustration of a financial crisis. Haunted by their challenges, most people tend to crack and consequently move away from God.

The real problem arises when a man tries to take everything into his own hands and feels that only he can pull himself out of the mess. While self-reliance is much appreciated, it is important to realize that no matter how able or how strong we are, we are nothing but mortal creatures. We need help and guidance from the Lord, and without his help, we can't even move a muscle.

It is important to have faith at all times, but it is even more important when everything fails, and it feels as if all the doors are closing on you. There are times when the path ahead seems dark. That is when we need to surrender to our maker and kneel down before him. He is the one that has sent us to this world, and surely he knows the answer to our problems and the cure to our pain. Our deliverance lies in being strong enough to have unshakable faith in the power of God.

Dealing with financial problems can be nerve-wracking, especially when you have a family to provide for. I have listed down a couple of ways to maneuver through financial worries without losing your faith out of frustration.

Let God Handle Your Fears and Anxieties

God is our refuge and strength, an ever-present help in trouble. Therefore, we will not fear. Psalm 46:1–2 (NIV)

While finances aren't easy to deal with, the pandemic has made it even more challenging even for the financially fit individuals to live in a carefree fashion as they used to. With lockdowns and restrictions, businesses all over the world have met their demise. In such trying times , it is perfectly normal for people to develop fears and anxieties. These fears and anxieties can pave the way for a sheer amount of hopelessness, which, if not addressed, can take the form of depression, and it has.

People have changed, their personalities have changed, their lifestyles have changed and their way of looking at life has also changed, and it is not for the better either. Some people even resort to drugs and alcohol to shy away from the problems. In my opinion, turning to intoxication is nothing but an ostrich approach. Christ doesn't want you to be weak. He doesn't want you to drown your sorrows by resorting to intoxications. He wants his people to be warriors, and the only thing that guides a warrior, besides his audacity, is an unwithering faith in the power of the Lord.

If you are dealing with financial stress after the pandemic, I would very much recommend seeing a therapist, for I don't want any of your mental problems to worsen. But I also advise sharing your issues with God. By sharing your problems with God, you will get a sense of relaxation that you won't find anywhere else. You won't find it in worldly pleasures, you won't find it in sex, and you won't find it in drugs either.

The first thing you need to do is to convince yourself that God truly loved us, and he cares about our problems more than we care about them. And, if you think God is far away, shake that thought as quickly as possible. God is right there with you, watching you, protecting you, and keeping problems at bay. Have you ever thought about all the things that could have happened to you but didn't? Why do you think those things haven't happened yet? It is because God doesn't want them to happen to you. Also, the financial worries that you are battling with at the moment have been sent onto you as a test from God.

The question is, are you willing to hand over your problems to him or not? Trust me, the day you start sharing your problems with God the same way you would do with your best friend, that is the day you will find not only peace but also the strength to cope with whatever comes your way.

Trust Him with Your Money

You may say to yourself, "My power and the strength of my hands have produced this wealth for me." But remember the Lord your God, for it is he who gives you the ability to produce wealth. Deuteronomy 8:17–18 (NIV)

There is one age-old concept that I want to share with you, and that is the idea of stewardship. Stewardship means taking care of and managing something that is not yours. Stewardship could be managing a department, a team of people, or some valuable resources at the behest of your clients or your employers.

Do you know where we are headed with the idea of stewardship? Yes, my friend, you have guessed it right. You have been sent to this world as God's steward. Whatever money you have right now is the money that has been handed over to you by God, and now it is your job to take care of it. It doesn't mean that you should quit your job right away.

You should execute your roles with great devotion, as it is a means of income that God chose for you. But, you must always remember that God is your provider and your sustainer. If it wasn't for his will, you wouldn't be able to secure a job nor make a single penny, no matter how hard you tried. What you need to do is to execute your job with the utmost diligence, and remember that God, who has taken care of you till here, will look after you going forward.

Trust in God's power to provide is one of the pillars on which our faith stands. In order to have a peaceful and calm life, it is important to do your job well and not worry about what will happen the day after. Either God will make things simpler for you, or even if they don't get too simple, he will find a way for you to deal with them more effectively than you can ever imagine. Such confidence in the power of God is necessary for living a fulfilling life.

Know You Are Dependent On God

Therefore I tell you, do not worry about your life. Look at the birds of the air; they do not sow or reap or store away in barns, and yet your heavenly Father feeds them. Are you not much more valuable than they? Matthew 6:25–27 (NIV)

Let's build up on the verses I have shared above. It is perfectly natural for a human to feel overwhelmed by financial worries. But, there is one thing that I want you to do every time you feel too burdened with finances. Every once in a while, spare a moment and take yourself to a place where no one goes. It could be an empty green field, a hilltop, or a beach that isn't too crowded.

Such desolate places allow you to disconnect from the urban hustle bustle, and connect with yourself on a deeper level. Once you reach such a spot, I want you to sit on the ground with your shoes off. I want you to look at the countless birds in the sky and the cattle that graze in the fields. Where do you think their food comes from? It comes from the same place your food comes from. It comes from the same God that created this earth and the numerous creations on it.

Now, have you found your answer? You, my friend, are no different from the birds and the cattle. No matter what your accolades are, at the end of the day, you are dependent on no one other than your maker. Without his will, nothing can come to you, and similarly, nothing can be taken away from you. It is fruitless to worry about something that hasn't happened yet. But somehow, we have been conditioned to worry about almost everything we are faced with, and even the things that we might never have to face ever.

We live in a world that is governed by laws that are so stringent that they compel a person to drift away from God. These laws are created by a bunch of people sitting at the top, which are no different from you and me. But because they are in a position of power, they take it upon themselves to play God and govern the people according to their whims and desires. Sadly, we are so impressionable and so gullible that we believe everything said to us as the gospel. It is a good thing to live by the rules, but the sad part is, somewhere inside, we also want to be in a position of power.

As we move up in the hierarchy, we continue to move further away from the Lord. We start believing that we are in control of our own lives, and only we have the power to choose what's best for us. But it doesn't happen that way. No matter how high you rise through the ranks, in the eyes of God, you are not even superior to a fly, and at each step, you will have to turn to him for help and guidance.

Part of the reason why so many people struggle is that they never fully come to terms with the idea of submission. We are so scared of life that we never allow ourselves to be fully vulnerable. We choose to stay so uptight all the time, hoping that it will somehow help us exercise control over our lives. This behavior affects not only our relationship with God but also the relationship we share with our fellow men.

What I want you to understand is that no matter what position you secure, you will always be dependent on God. Whether you become the CEO of the world's largest MNC or the president of the United States, there will come a time when you will be forced to kneel before the Lord and ask for his help. So might as well do it willingly because when it's the other way around, it's not easy for a person to handle.

I believe the easiest way to let the idea of dependency really sink in is through humility. The road to humility isn't easy, but it is possible. So, start doing small things like helping a person in need or feeding a stray. By doing these small tasks, you will find it easier to attain the nearness of God, and then you won't have a hard time depending on God for the things that are out of your hands.

Practice Contentment

I have learned the secret of being content in any and every situation, whether well fed or hungry, whether living in plenty or in want. I can do all this through him, who gives me strength. Philippians 4:12–13 (NIV)

Alright, this may seem a little counterintuitive to what we discussed in the beginning of this book. In the beginning, we spoke of being wealthy, as well as the passive income streams that can help us embark on the journey towards financial independence. There are a few things that I want you to understand.

First of all, working for financial success and the urge to become wealthy is not a bad thing. In fact, it is necessary, considering the nature of the world. You and I are products of the same system that thrives on the urge to make money. Moreover, a person that is financially fit can use their status to contribute for the betterment of society.

What I want you to understand is that although being wealthy is important, it isn't the primary objective of human existence. Since the day we open our eyes, we are conditioned to chase after wealth, as if that is what our time on earth is all about, while it's not. What's even sadder is that the more wealth we accumulate, we tend to become greedier, and it's even scarier to realize that this greed never fully goes away unless we choose to make some serious changes to the way we think and the way we see the world.

One of the many things that distinguish between a believer and a non-believer is that a believer is content with whatever he has. He is grateful for whatever blessings God has bestowed upon him, and he doesn't spend his days stressing over ways to enhance his riches. He considers himself fortunate enough to own whatever little that he has. People who can conjure such a mindset find it easier to get closer to the Lord, thus living a life that is free of stress and anxiety.

"Naked I came from my mother's womb, and naked I will depart. The Lord gave, and the Lord has taken away; may the name of the Lord be praised." Job 1:21 (NIV)

A believer doesn't spend his days trying harder than necessary to flaunt his material gains to this mortal world. His primary ambition is to fulfill the commandments of the Lord. He knows well enough that no matter how much riches he accumulates, a day will come when he will have to leave, and none of his Ferraris or his iPhones will be of any use.

He spends his time in pious contemplation and making efforts to contribute to the betterment of mankind, and nothing else is more important to him. He believes utterly in the power of good deeds and the impact they will have on what becomes of him in the afterlife. To him, securing a powerful place in paradise is far more important than fulfilling his worldly desires. Even if he has to live a difficult life, he will do so willingly if it helps him closer to the Lord.

Moreover, he doesn't compare himself to other people in terms of worldly gains. Instead, he follows the path of our Lord and Savior, Jesus Christ. He spends his days and nights trying to follow in Christ's footsteps. Half of his time is spent in prayer, while the rest of his time is spent doing good deeds and helping those in need.

Another thing that distinguishes between a believer and a non-believer is that a believer will find a way to help the needy, even if his own survival is uncertain. A non-believer, on the other hand, will always have an excuse not to help. The choice is yours. You have to decide which category you fall into.

The easiest way, in my opinion, to defeat any financial worries is by inculcating contentment in your life. Don't forget to praise the Lord, and always thank him for whatever he has given you. From an emotional aspect, it will free you from whatever financial worries you deal with every day. From a financial viewpoint, the day you start practicing contentment, God will open the doors of abundance upon you, and you will be amazed at the favors he will bestow upon you out of His grace.

Be Generous

This is how we know what love is: Jesus Christ laid down his life for us. And we ought to lay down our lives for our brothers and sisters. Dear children, let us not love with words or speech but with actions and in truth. 1 John 3:16–18 (NIV)

This is the stage where it gets more fun. If you can master the first four tips I have shared with you, you won't have a hard time splurging for the better of those around you. Moreover, you will also find it easier to enjoy your money without ever being controlled by it. As we have discussed above, if you are generous and kind, you will be amazed at the sheer amount of God's generosity that is extended your way.

Think of the time you bought a nice Christmas present for your child. The happiness your child felt at that very moment must have lit up your world. That's how parents are wired. They will go to extreme lengths to provide for their children. Parents have no issue spending on their children, and the best part is, they don't expect anything in return.

Now, think of the level of generosity God shows to his people. It may sound strange, but God loves his creation a hundred times more than a mother loves her child. Do you think God won't reward you for being generous towards his creation? He will reward you more than you can even think of.

So help the helpless, and one day when you feel helpless, he will send help in his own unique ways and at a time that he chooses for you. And, if you think God doesn't notice your generosity, you need to think again. God knows you and everything you do like the back of your hand. Your generosity will be rewarded in ways that are beyond your expectation.

In the beginning, you will have a hard time setting aside a sum of money for other people, and there is nothing to be ashamed about. After all, you are human, and especially in the post-pandemic economy, one has to think twice before making a decision that is financial in nature. So, every time you don't feel generous enough, tell yourself that whatever money you spend isn't yours to begin with. It has been given to you by God, and it is your duty towards your maker to spend on his creation. Moreover, you should feel grateful that God chose you to help others. That in itself is a blessing.

When you practice generosity, don't just think about the material rewards God will bestow upon you. Think of all the sins that he will wash away and how they will help you on the Day of

Judgment. Generosity is not something you can develop overnight. Instead, it is a mindset that you cultivate with some honest self-reflection, your inner goodness, and some life experiences that are extremely important.

www.ingramcontent.com/pod-product-compliance
Lightning Source LLC
LaVergne TN
LVHW022216200926
848481LV00006B/1986